Strike Up the

CW00555765

A comedy

Olwen Wymark

Samuel French – London
New York – Sydney – Toronto – Hollywood

CHARACTERS

Mrs Carmichael
Geraldine Stringer, her daughter
Reg Stringer, her husband
Billie Stringer, their daughter
Mr Beamish
Bunny Beamish, his son

The action takes place in the living-room of the Stringers' house somewhere in the Green Belt

ACT I   5 a.m.

ACT II   Later that evening

Time—the present

ACT I

The living-room of the Stringers' house somewhere in the Green Belt. 5 a.m.

There are two doors, one to the kitchen and one to the front hall. The furniture comprises a three-piece suite, a large cupboard and a sideboard. There is a mirror on one wall, and various pictures on the others

Music: "Strike Up the Band"

The Lights come up on Mrs Carmichael hoovering the living-room. The curtains are drawn and the light is on. In her sixties, dressed in a smart suit and fur piece, Mrs Carmichael works with speed and a graceful ferocity, manipulating the hoover with one hand and shifting the furniture to clean under it with the other

Geraldine Stringer comes running wildly on, dressed in her nightgown and fastening her dressing-gown. She sees Mrs Carmichael, who doesn't see her, registers consternation and starts to tiptoe out

Mrs Carmichael, unable to shift one of the armchairs with one hand, switches off the hoover. Geraldine, her back to her, freezes. Mrs Carmichael addresses the chair sternly

Mrs Carmichael Will you move!
Geraldine (*panicking*) Move?

Mrs Carmichael screams and they whip round to face each other

Mrs Carmichael Geraldine, how could you!
Geraldine How could I what?
Mrs Carmichael Creep up on me like that. (*She collapses into a chair*)
Geraldine But Mother——
Mrs Carmichael Always such a thoughtless girl. I feel I failed with you. Handbag.
Geraldine (*handing it to her*) Will you just tell me why——
Mrs Carmichael (*getting out pills*) Glass of water.
Geraldine Mother, it is five a.m.!
Mrs Carmichael Don't bellow at me please. I've had a shock. Besides, it isn't. It was nearly quarter-past when I got here.
Geraldine But why get here at all? Why are you hoovering the carpet? Why aren't you in Colchester?
Mrs Carmichael Water, Geraldine, please!
Geraldine Oh all right.

Geraldine goes out

Mrs Carmichael (*calling*) I realized I had time to pop in here before my train. The opening session of the conference isn't till nine. Billie let me in. I've sent her to my house for some plants. Did you know your Japanese azalea was dead?

Geraldine comes in with a glass of water

Geraldine Yes. Mother, why are you here?

Mrs Carmichael Well Geraldine, we don't want Mr Beamish coming into a pigsty. Thank you, dear. It's simply a question of careful watering, constant temperature and talking to them. Did you ever talk to that azalea?

Geraldine I don't speak Japanese. What do you mean, pigsty? Mrs Fisher was here for three hours yesterday. I think it looks very nice.

Mrs Carmichael Your standards have gone down and down since you married that man. God knows I warned you ... oh, and I would like to know about this. (*She gets a black bag out from behind the sofa*)

Geraldine It's just some jumble. There's a sale this week.

Mrs Carmichael (*pulling things out of the bag*) I cannot believe you mean to throw this away!

Geraldine Reg's old jacket? But you always said it was common.

Mrs Carmichael (*holding it up*) Very common. Reginald has appalling taste. You should never let him choose his own clothes. (*She throws the jacket aside*) No I meant this. The Jaeger skirt I bought you.

Geraldine Mother, it doesn't fit me.

Mrs Carmichael Nonsense, of course it does. And it would go beautifully with the white angora sweater I knitted you—which I never see you wearing by the way——

Geraldine (*hastily*) What are these—tranquillizers?

Mrs Carmichael Certainly not. Vitamin E14. They coat the nerve endings. Tranquillizers are the enemy of the family. Single parents, peace marchers, feminists—all on tranquillizers. I'm leading a discussion on it at the conference. What are you wearing tonight?

Geraldine My sequin sleeveless.

Mrs Carmichael No no, dear, absolutely not. You'd give quite the wrong impression. That long black skirt I think, don't you, and a nice blouse.

Geraldine I don't see any reason at all why I shouldn't——

Mrs Carmichael By the way, I'm sorry to have to tell you that Mrs Fisher hoovers round as I've always suspected. Well, I'll just check the dining-room before my taxi arrives. (*She starts towards the kitchen*)

Geraldine Honestly, Mother, there's no need for——

Mrs Carmichael Such a terrible misfortune that the one time Mr Beamish was free to come to dinner should be the day of my Colchester conference.

Mrs Carmichael goes out to the kitchen

(*As she goes*) If I hadn't been the main speaker tonight I would certainly have considered cancelling. (*She screams*)

She comes back carrying a frozen turkey thawing in a pan

What is this?

Geraldine (*sulkily*) It's a turkey.

Mrs Carmichael Fricassee of veal!

Geraldine Yes I know but——

Mrs Carmichael We went through every single one of your cookbooks and we finally decided——

Geraldine We . . . ha!

Mrs Carmichael (*ignoring this*)—that fricassee of veal was the perfect solution. Elegant but not pretentious.

Geraldine The butcher didn't have any veal.

Mrs Carmichael I shall phone my own butcher at once.

Geraldine You can't. He won't be open yet.

Mrs Carmichael I always telephone him at home.

Geraldine Mother, I've never cooked it before. I haven't had any practice. It might be a total disaster and I——

Mrs Carmichael There's no need to get emotional and hyperbolic, Geraldine, though it is true you are not a good cook, I shall never know why. (*She sighs*) Turkey . . . you are giving him the leek and pumpkin soup for starters?

Geraldine (*bravely*) Prawn cocktail.

Mrs Carmichael (*in horror*) Prawn cocktail! (*After a pause; grimly*) And the lemon soufflé?

Geraldine Strawberries.

Mrs Carmichael (*after a pause*) I see. (*Silence*)

Geraldine (*nervously*) Mother?

Mrs Carmichael picks up her handbag and starts out

You're not going. Oh honestly, there's no need to get into a state just because——

Mrs Carmichael Just because? Just because my own daughter my only child, repudiates me? (*She resumes her exit*)

Geraldine Don't go, Mother. I didn't mean to hurt your feelings.

Mrs Carmichael (*turning; reproachfully*) How many thousand times have I heard you say that. Geraldine, I have lain awake night after night worrying about this dinner party.

Geraldine Reg told me Mr Beamish liked turkey. I was only——

Mrs Carmichael A moment. I'm thinking. Yes. You must tell Mr Beamish to carve.

Geraldine Why?

Mrs Carmichael Yes I can see it! Standing at the head of the table, sharpening the carving knife on the steel, the little family round him—perfect. The paterfamilias.

Geraldine Mother! He's only a guest!

Mrs Carmichael Mr Beamish isn't *only* anything. Apart from being your husband's employer and, I pray God, your daughter's future father-in-law, he is also a famous person. He appears on television.

Geraldine Appeared. Once. Waffling on about sex.

Mrs Carmichael No, really I despair of you. It's all this listening to Radio

Three and reading foreign novels. Waffling on? A man who has dedicated his life to guarding public morals? He gives up hours of his free time to monitor films and television. Voluntarily. Nobody asked him to.

Geraldine (*sotto voce*) Quite.

Mrs Carmichael And why? Because he sees it as his duty, a word we hear little enough nowadays. Do you know he writes letters to newspaper editors at the rate of up to a dozen a week? That he travels round the whole country giving talks to church groups? That he gives away free copies of the books he publishes to old-age pensioners?

Geraldine (*closing her eyes*) Yes ... yes ... yes.

Mrs Carmichael Oh when I think how lucky you are! Billie on the verge of a wonderful future—and here you are slopping about in your dressing-gown as usual.

Geraldine I was in bed!

Mrs Carmichael Whereas I had to watch *my* daughter throw herself away

Geraldine groans

on an irresponsible ne'er-do-well. A Hippie Person who thought he could make a living publishing disgusting books only fit for lunatics and drug addicts. I couldn't hold my head up in the streets.

Geraldine He did make a living. We were quite well off.

Mrs Carmichael Then why did he take you to live in the slums?

Geraldine Mother, for the thousandth time, Islington was not the slums.

Mrs Carmichael My granddaughter ... a deprived child.

Geraldine She wasn't deprived. Reg was very successful.

Mrs Carmichael Did he or did he not go bankrupt?

Geraldine It was the recession. Lots of people went bankrupt.

Mrs Carmichael Not Mr Beamish.

Geraldine No.

Mrs Carmichael And let us thank God that when he bought up Reginald's firm he bought Reginald too.

Geraldine He didn't buy him! He simply gave him a——

Mrs Carmichael And why did Mr Beamish not go bankrupt? Because the books he publishes are wholesome and constructive and good for people.

Geraldine And boring.

Mrs Carmichael (*after a pause*) I am wasting my breath. I can see I'm not wanted here.

She picks up her bag again and starts out

Billie comes in from the hall leading to the front door. She wears a nightgown, anorak and wellingtons. She's carrying a pot plant

Billie Granny, I couldn't get them all——Morning, Mother. You're up early.

Geraldine Yes.

Billie Only five of them would fit in the car, Granny. Do you think that'll be enough?

Mrs Carmichael Take them back, Billie. Your mother doesn't want my help.

Billie (*cheerfully*) Yes she does, Granny. She was only saying yesterday how she wished you could be here tonight.

Billie goes out again

Geraldine You see?

Mrs Carmichael What I see is a sweet child shielding her mother. A thing you never never did for me.

Geraldine (*confused*) What?

Mrs Carmichael All through your teens you did nothing but chafe and complain and criticize me . . .

Geraldine Oh my God!

Mrs Carmichael Don't blaspheme, Geraldine. I'm leaving.

She starts out again

Billie comes in with more plants

Geraldine Billie, will you please tell your grandmother to stay.

Billie Stay, Granny. Should I put all the plants in the dining-room? Granny thinks we should mitigate the kitchen aspect of the kitchen/dining-room.

Billie goes out again

Geraldine (*warmly*) Oh does she?

Mrs Carmichael Goodbye, Geraldine. I won't be coming back. Billie can visit me at my house if you have no objections. I shall simply——

Geraldine (*wildly*) Mother, I beg you, I implore you to stay! I'm sorry I upset you, it was wonderful of you to find the time to come over. I really do appreciate it . . . please stay!

Mrs Carmichael pauses. She inclines her head submissively and sits

Mrs Carmichael (*briskly*) Now about these strawberries. (*She gets out a notebook*) It would be the work of a moment to whip up a zabaglione to go with them. How many eggs have you got?

Geraldine Uh . . . two. No, three I think.

Mrs Carmichael (*writing*) The mark of the genuine homemaker is at least eight eggs in the larder at all times.

Geraldine Oh well I'll go and buy five more.

Mrs Carmichael Yes. And you'll need a bottle of marsala. Four desert-spoonfuls of caster sugar and——

Billie comes in with more plants

Billie Your taxi's here, Granny.

Mrs Carmichael Oh isn't that annoying. I shall have to go. I mustn't miss that train. (*She starts out, then stops*) Oh. I nearly forgot.

She gets a brown wig out of her handbag and holds it up to her head as she looks in the mirror. She rejects it. She gets a blue-rinse wig out and puts it on. Billie and Geraldine stare

Geraldine Mother?

Mrs Carmichael (*busy*) Yes dear?

Geraldine Why are you wearing that wig?

Mrs Carmichael I spent a great deal of money on this perm. I don't want it blown to bits on the journey. Couldn't make up my mind between the brown and the blue rinse but I really think——

Billie (*troubled*) Granny ...

Mrs Carmichael Mmm?

Billie It makes you look ... American.

Mrs Carmichael You think so?

Billie (*ruefully*) Yes I do.

Mrs Carmichael (*a shrewd glance in the mirror*) Point taken, Billie. (*She gets out a scarf*) I don't care for headscarves—except for the Royals, naturally. Still, I won't be meeting anyone I know. Good gracious, is that the time? (*She checks her watch*) No. (*Reprovingly to the clock*) Wrong. (*She starts out*) I'll ring from Colchester and dictate the zabaglione recipe to you, Geraldine.

Geraldine Thank you, Mother.

Mrs Carmichael Oh dear, there were dozens of other things I wanted to say. The canapés—remember to grill the mushrooms on a very low flame.

Geraldine Yes.

Mrs Carmichael And not peanuts, Geraldine, cashews. Well worth the extra expense.

Geraldine Yes.

Mrs Carmichael He almost certainly won't drink. You've got fruit juices? Perrier?

Geraldine Yes.

Mrs Carmichael You remembered to get the candles?

Geraldine Yes.

Mrs Carmichael Blue? To match the napkins?

Geraldine Yes!

Mrs Carmichael Do my chestnut and green olive stuffing for the turkey.

Geraldine (*beginning to crack*) Yes! I will!

Mrs Carmichael Billie, remember what I said about talking to much. Men like Mr Beamish never care for intellectual women.

Billie Yes, Granny. Right.

Mrs Carmichael Salad before the cheese. Don't forget.

Billie I won't.

Mrs Carmichael And finish the hoovering for me, dear. I didn't do under the armchairs.

Billie I will.

Mrs Carmichael I pray God it will be all right.

Billie Don't worry, Granny.

Mrs Carmichael It's the least I can do, child.

The taxi honks. During the above Geraldine has slumped gradually down into a prone position on the sofa, her eyes closed

(*She opens the door. A curt call to the taxi*) Be quiet! (*She takes Billie by the shoulders. In thrilling tones*) It matters not how strait the gate, Billie.

Billie (*lost*) What ... oh! How charged with punishments the scroll, Granny?

Mrs Carmichael Absolutely! I am the master of my fate! I am the captain of my soul! Remember that tonight, Billie. Goodbye!

Mrs Carmichael goes

Billie (*waving*) Goodbye, Granny. Goodbye. (*Getting the hoover*) Oh it's such a shame that Granny can't be here tonight.

Geraldine (*without moving*) Yes.

Billie She wouldn't have any trouble handling Mr Beamish.

Geraldine No.

Billie And then it would be three and three. You, me and Granny—Mr Beamish, Daddy and Bunny ... Oh God!

Geraldine (*starting up*) What? What's wrong?

Billie I forgot to ask Granny if we should have place cards.

Geraldine (*lying down again*) No, we shouldn't.

Billie You don't think Mr Beamish would expect them?

Geraldine No, I don't.

Billie (*worriedly*) Everything's got to be absolutely right tonight.

Geraldine It will be, it will be.

Billie I hope you're going to like Bunny.

Geraldine (*with eyes closed*) I'm sure I am.

Billie (*complacently*) He's an eccentric.

Geraldine Lovely.

Billie Mother ...

Geraldine Mmmm?

Billie Do you think marriage *per se* is a bar to personal autonomy?

Geraldine (*nearly asleep*) No, no ...

Billie Bunny thinks he thinks that. But I'm sure he doesn't really. And he goes on a lot about "ritual and hypocrisy" but I don't see anything intrinsically wrong with weddings myself. Proper ones I mean, not the registry office like you and Daddy. Poor Granny, she says she never could forgive you for that.

Geraldine (*eyes closed, smiling*) I know.

Billie Anyway the main thing about marriage is you know where you are. People living with people doesn't necessarily last. Is this turkey supposed to be here?

Geraldine Yes.

Billie Oh. But if they're married and they do happen to fall out of love with each other they still stay together. Like you and Daddy.

Geraldine Mmmm hmmm. (*She opens her eyes*) What do you mean, like me and Daddy?

Billie You know ... just accept it. Settle down. Daddy in his Homburg and all that. By the way, have you decided what you're going to wear tonight?

Geraldine The sequin sleeveless.

Billie (*alarmed*) Oh Mother, do you think you should try to look glamorous tonight? I mean that dress is very sort of—revealing, isn't it.

Geraldine Too young for me? Mutton dressed as lamb?

Billie Oh no. No. It's just that Mr Beamish is ultra conservative, Bunny says. Couldn't you wear your long black skirt and——

Geraldine (*snapping*) A nice blouse! That dress was a present from Reg as it happens and we have not "fallen out of love". That's a ridiculous thing to say.

Billie Well I know you're still very fond of each other.

Geraldine Oh thanks very much.

Billie But it's different from the old days. In London. When I was little.

Geraldine I don't know what you think you're talking about, Billie. Of course things are different. Times have changed. The world's changed but Reg and I have not changed!

Billie switches on the hoover

(*Raising her voice*) We feel exactly the same about each other as we always did and there is absolutely no need whatever for you to hoover the carpet, Mrs Fisher did it yesterday!

Billie Granny says Mrs Fisher hoovers round——

Geraldine (*with passion; switching off the hoover*) I know! I know! I know!

Billie (*a bit taken aback*) Anyway I've nearly finished. Then all I have to do is run round the skirting-board with a damp cloth.

Geraldine I can't stand it. I'm going back to bed!

Geraldine goes

Billie looks after her, shakes her head and switches on the hoover again as the Lights fade to Black-out. Music

Billie exits with the hoover

The Lights come up. It is later that morning

Reg, in dark suit and Homburg, trots across the stage from the kitchen. He's carrying some papers, which he's reading, and a tea cosy. Geraldine comes out of the kitchen holding his briefcase

Reg . . .

Reg Gerry, please! It's the wrong time of day for that conversation and I've got to present this paper to the board at——

Geraldine Reg.

Reg You know what I'm like in the morning. Can't you——

She holds up the briefcase. He looks at the tea cosy with amazement. They swap

Geraldine I was only telling you what Billie said.

Reg Yes, well Billie's views on love and marriage are bound to be . . . Oh God!

Geraldine What? What's wrong?

Reg You reminded me yesterday to buy the champagne for the toast tonight and I've just remembered I forgot. What are we going to——

Geraldine Reg. You reminded *me* to buy the champagne. And I did.

Reg Did I? Did you? Oh good. That's a relief.

Geraldine And sherry and whisky and claret, though he almost certainly doesn't drink. And in most households the man is in charge of all that.

Reg (*interested*) You sound just like your mother.

Geraldine I do not! Take that back!

Reg I take it back. I'm going to be late. (*He sees the turkey*) What's this . . . ?

Geraldine Mother was here this morning.

Reg (*in horror*) Here? Today? Why? You said she was going to Colchester. You swore to me you'd picked a night she'd be out of town. You promised me! (*He looks round apprehensively*) Where is she now?

Geraldine She did go. She caught an early train.

Reg Thank God.

Geraldine You're terrified of my mother.

Reg (*surprised*) Of course. Well . . . goodbye, dear.

He kisses her on the cheek and starts to go. She stops him

Geraldine Reg, do you think we've turned into a typical suburban couple.

Reg Of course not. Don't be ridiculous.

Geraldine Busy little commuter? Boring little housewife?

Reg (*laughing*) Oh Gerry, nobody could ever call you boring. (*After a pause*) Or a housewife.

Geraldine Reg! You agree with her!

Reg Who?

Geraldine Mother.

Reg No!

Geraldine Yes! You just said! Hopeless housewife.

Reg I didn't, you're not and I'm going to miss my bus.

Geraldine I suppose that's my fault too. I do everything wrong, don't I? The wrong food, the wrong charlady, the wrong kitchen/dining-room——

Reg What are you talking about?

Geraldine And no doubt you think the sequin sleeveless is the wrong dress for tonight too!

Reg Tonight? Oh. Well. Uh . . . you look marvellous in that dress, Gerry, but——

Geraldine But what?

Reg Is it a mother-in-law's dress?

Geraldine I am not a mother-in-law. I am a person! And I'd like to know why everybody is so dead set on me looking dowdy and stodgy and boring and——

Reg Now, Gerry, nobody wants you to . . . oh my God, is that the time?

Geraldine No.

Reg What?

Geraldine That clock is twenty-five minutes fast. In the mornings.

Reg Really? Only in the mornings? That's very——

Geraldine How else would you get you off to the bus stop if you were me?

Reg Oh right. Yes, I can see that. Well. Bit of time in hand. There were a couple of things I wanted to mention about tonight.

Geraldine Oh yes?

Reg Just a few little pointers for you.

Geraldine Go on.

Reg Jokes. Don't make any. Mr Beamish has no sense of humour. Topics of conversation: there are many no-go areas, e.g. modern art, alternative medicine, equal rights, unilateral disarmament ... in fact avoid politics altogether. Mr Beamish is so far right of centre you'd need a telescope to see him. Which reminds me, keep in focus when he's talking to you.

Geraldine In what?

Reg Focus. He's as blind as a bat but he won't admit it. He only has one pair of spectacles and they're reading glasses. What else? What else? Oh yes, punctuality. He's completely obsessed so be sure dinner's on time. (*After a pause*) I think that's everything.

Geraldine Quite sure?

Reg Hope so. It's absolutely crucial that we get everything right. You don't know how crucial.

Geraldine (*manic*) Oh I do, Reg, I do I do! I only hope I can live up to it all!

Reg Geraldine, if anybody could live up to anything it would probably be you.

Geraldine (*fiercely*) And what's that supposed to mean?

Reg Nothing. I was only——

Geraldine You stand there in that hat——

Reg What's my hat got to do with it?

Geraldine You wouldn't have been seen dead in a Homburg ten years ago. Billie's right. You have changed. And you love it, don't you. Nine to five at the office, kotowing to the boss, living in the Green Belt ...

Reg I do not love it and we live in the bloody Green Belt because your mother told us to and she lent us the money for the deposit!

Geraldine You could have said no.

Reg So could you.

Geraldine You're the man.

Reg All right. And the man earns the money to pay the mortgage, yes?

Geraldine So why didn't you find a better job?

Reg I tried!

Geraldine Not hard enough!

Reg By God, it's true. You are a bully.

Geraldine And you're pathetic.

Reg Thanks so much.

Geraldine You used to be funny.

Reg You used to be nice. (*He starts out*) I'm going to be late to the office.

Geraldine So be late. In the old days you were never on time for anything.

Reg (*angrily*) You want me to lose this job, don't you? You'll be glad if he does make me redundant.

Geraldine What? That man is giving you the sack? All these years in a boring underpaid stupid job that you hate——

Reg I don't hate it.

Geraldine You do!

Reg Yes I do. I don't want to talk about it. It's probably only a rumour. He hasn't actually said anything about——

Geraldine Well, ask him! Go straight into his office this morning and——

Reg Are you insane? Mr Beamish is not the kind of person you can——
Geraldine Reg! He walks all over you because you let him. You have to fight back! You have to——
Reg Will you shut up? Can't you see if this engagement thing does come off he won't be able to sack me.
Geraldine (*drama*) Dear God! You'd sacrifice your only child just to save your paltry little——
Reg I'm not sacrificing anybody! She's in love with him.
Geraldine (*triumphantly*) Yes! But she might easily not have been.
Reg (*after a brief pause*) Right. Yes. Good point. I'm going.
Geraldine You're not going to speak to him about your job, is that it?
Reg That's it.
Geraldine You refuse to face up to him and be a man?
Reg I do.

Reg goes

Geraldine (*starting after him; furious*) Reg——

The sound of the front door slamming shut. She trips over the sports jacket still on the floor, picks it up and starts to shove it savagely into the bag. She stops, holds it up, looks at it

(*With narrowed eyes*) Oh you do, do you? (*She tucks the jacket under her arm*)

The Lights fade as she starts to drag the jumble out towards the hall. Blackout. Music

Geraldine exits

The Lights come up. It is evening

Billie comes in dressed up

She goes busily round the room straightening things, etc. Then she sighs elaborately

Billie (*calling towards the stairs*) Mother? Aren't you ready yet?
Geraldine (*off, from upstairs*) Not quite, darling.
Billie (*beady*) Why are you taking so long?
Geraldine (*off*) Well I want to look my best, don't I.
Billie Shall I come up and help you?
Geraldine (*off, sharply*) No! (*Then recovering herself*) No need thank you, dear. By the way there's a little problem.
Billie (*tense*) What do you mean? What problem?
Geraldine (*off*) I forgot to buy the marsala.
Billie Oh my God! How can we make the zabaglione?
Geraldine (*off*) Could you pop down to the off-licence?
Billie I can't! How can I? They'll be here any minute.
Geraldine (*off*) I forgot to tell you. They're not arriving till eight.
Billie (*off*) Eight? Daddy told me seven-thirty sharp.

Geraldine (*off*) Little change of plan. He phoned from the office. Off you go, there's a good girl. You've got half an hour.

Billie Why can't you go?

Geraldine (*off*) Because I'm changing.

Billie (*starting out*) Honestly! You're always forgetting things.

Billie goes out through the kitchen

We hear the back door shut. Geraldine sings "If You Were the Only Boy in the World". The front door opens. She stops abruptly

Reg (*off, calling*) Mr Beamish. (*After a pause, louder*) I say!

Mr Beamish (*off, further away*) What is it, Stringer? What are you doing over there?

Reg (*off*) I live here, Mr Beamish. This is our house.

Mr Beamish (*off, closer*) Are you sure?

Reg (*off*) Oh absolutely positive. I'd know it anywhere. Do come in.

They enter. Mr Beamish is also in a dark suit and Homburg and carries an umbrella and a briefcase

Mr Beamish In that case, whose house is that?

Reg It belongs to a Mr and Mrs Blick, Mr Beamish. Recently moved here from Cirencester. A very charming couple. Three children. Two girls and a boy—and the rabbit, of course.

Mr Beamish I wonder you didn't indicate the correct house while I was instructing my chauffeur how to park the car.

Reg I didn't like to interrupt.

Mr Beamish (*disapproving*) You say you breed rabbits?

Reg No. No indeed not, Mr Beamish, no. Well . . . as a boy many years ago. At present we have only the bird and the tortoise.

Mr Beamish And the one child, am I right?

Reg Absolutely right. Yes. (*After a pause*) Well well, I wonder where everybody's got to. (*He goes towards the stairs and calls with casual urgency*) Geraldine? Billie! (*He pauses*) Oh. Kitchen, of course. (*He sprints to the kitchen door*) Billie! Geraldine!

Mr Beamish Your family would appear to have gone out.

Reg Impossible. Unthinkable, Mr Beamish, I assure you. I can't tell you how excited they've been about your coming tonight.

Mr Beamish (*complacently*) Is that so?

Reg My goodness yes. They've thought about nothing else for days.

Mr Beamish Well, we might be a shade early. (*He looks at his watch*) Yes. Seven-twenty-seven. It may be that they are in fact upstairs. Behind closed doors. Out of earshot. Last minute titivations.

Reg That'll be it of course. Mr Beamish, let me take your things.

Mr Beamish (*giving them to Reg*) You may wonder, Stringer, why I don't leave my briefcase in the car.

Reg (*balancing it all with difficulty*) Well . . .

Mr Beamish (*lowered tones*) It's my belief that my chauffeur picks the lock and reads all my papers.

Reg No!

Mr Beamish He may well be a mole for a rival publisher.

Reg Good heavens!

Mr Beamish When did we launch our new How-To Books?

Reg Third week of January, wasn't it?

Mr Beamish Exactly. And one week before that launch didn't Challenger Books bring out one of *our* best titles? *How To Adjust To Poverty?*

Reg That's true! And you think your driver . . .

Mr Beamish I have no hard evidence as yet but I watch him like a hawk.

Reg turns to put Mr Beamish's things into a cupboard which he has trouble getting open. Mr Beamish peers disapprovingly at a picture

Geraldine comes in and stands smiling in the doorway from the hall. She's dressed like a man in Reg's sports jacket, a wig and a moustache

Mr Beamish turns and sees her

Er—how do you do.

Reg Oh jolly good. Here you are.

Reg turns round and sees her. He stands stock still holding Mr Beamish's things. He is riven with horror and shock

Geraldine (*expansively*) Pleased to meet you. I'm Rollo Stringer. Reginald's brother.

Reg (*strangulated outrage*) I haven't got a brother!

Geraldine (*clapping him on the back*) Ah Reginald, Reginald . . . can't we let bygones by bygones? (*Ruefully to Mr Beamish*) An old wound, a boyhood rift—still unhealed. Here Reg, let me help you with those things, eh?

She takes Mr Beamish's things from him and chucks them into the cupboard. She turns to Reg

All right, old man?

Reg (*hysterically*) Geraldine!

Geraldine Ah. Geraldine. Just rushing out as I came in. Off to see our mama. I gather the old lady's not quite the ticket.

Mr Beamish I'm sorry. I had looked forward to meeting her.

Geraldine Really? Our mother? She's nearly eighty-nine. Oh I am a jackass. You mean Geraldine. She may be back.

The phone rings

That might be her now, Reg.

Reg (*convulsively*) What?

Geraldine Geraldine. That may be her now. On the phone.

Reg (*helplessly*) Yes you're right. Geraldine. What? On the phone. Yes. Why not? Certainly. (*He picks up the phone*) Hello. Sorry, wrong number. (*He hangs up. He smiles brilliantly at Mr Beamish*) Such a bore. The telephone system in this country. Archaic!

The phone rings again

(*He picks it up*) Hello. Hello. . . . Who? . . . What? I can't hear you.

Geraldine (*helpfully*) Shall I speak to them?

Reg (*a near scream*) No! (*To the phone*) Sorry. Who? . . . Oh. It's for you. Mr Beamish.

Mr Beamish For me? Who is it?·

Reg Bun.

Geraldine Bun?

Mr Beamish My son.

Geraldine All my buns, eh? (*She laughs heartily*)

Mr Beamish (*regarding her briefly; sharply to Reg*) But why is he telephoning? He should be here.

Reg I don't know!

Mr Beamish (*taking the phone*) Yes, Bun? What is it?

Reg (*agonized undertone to Geraldine*) Why? Why?

Geraldine Have a cigar.

Reg Go and change!

Geraldine But I just have.

Mr Beamish (*into the phone*) I will send my chaffeur. Where shall he——what?

Reg Have you gone mad?

Geraldine Not mad, macho. Don't you like it?

Mr Beamish (*into the phone*) No, I fail to see how your socialist principles prevent you from having a lift in the Rolls . . . What? What's that?

Reg (*urgently*) What are we going to do? What can we do? How am I going to explain?

Geraldine Oh don't be so neurotic, Reg. It was just a bit of fun. I'm going to change back in a minute.

Reg Fun!

Mr Beamish (*into the phone*) Bun, I do not wish to argue the point. Simply tell me the name of the street. (*He writes it down*) Yes . . . yes . . .

Reg He's bound to realize. Bound to!

Geraldine You said he was blind as a bat. Relax, Reg.

Reg Relax!

Mr Beamish (*into the phone*) Right you are. Goodbye. (*To Reg*) Bun has asked if your daughter might drive over and pick him up. I have the address here.

Reg Yes, of course. Certainly.

The sound of the back door

(*Panicking*) What's that?

Geraldine (*moving with careful speed towards the stairs*) I think that will be Billie now.

Reg moans

Mr Beamish Ah. Good timing.

Geraldine Absolutely. Go and tell her, eh Reg? (*She pauses, then beams at him*) Or shall I? (*She makes a move*)

Reg (*another strangled scream*) No! (*He races for the kitchen*) No, no! I will!

*He stops and looks despairingly at Geraldine. He makes flapping motions at
her with his hands. She waves back. He groans, races for the door again, stops,
races back*

He seizes the piece of paper from Mr Beamish and races out

Geraldine Dear old Reg. Always on the move.
Mr Beamish Yes . . . he is certainly more volatile here in his own home than
we generally find him at the office.
Geraldine (*comfortably*) Anxious perhaps about Geraldine.
Mr Beamish Anxious?
Geraldine He is always a little lost without her, I find.
Mr Beamish But surely she will be returning soon?
Geraldine (*cryptically*) We can but hope. Geraldine is a mysterious and
passionate woman, Mr Beamish.
Mr Beamish What makes you say that?
Geraldine My own knowledge of her. My own very deep knowledge of her.
Mr Beamish I'm not sure I——
Geraldine Quite frankly Mr Beamish, I couldn't live without her.
Mr Beamish (*in horror*) What are you telling me?
Geraldine (*winking*) Oh come now. Both men of the world, eh?
Mr Beamish (*outraged*) Mr Stringer!

Reg appears suddenly from the kitchen

Reg Yes? (*He breathes heavily for a moment*) Billie has left in the Morris to
collect Bunny. (*He hands Geraldine a bottle*) She said to give you this.
Geraldine Jolly kind. Marsala, eh? Mr B and I have been having a bit of the
old changing-room chat, eh Beamish old man? (*She nudges him in the ribs*)
Reg (*involuntary fury*) Geraldine!
Geraldine (*after a pause; enthusiastically*) Oh, is she back? Splendid! (*She
goes towards the hall*) Gerry? Mr Beamish and Reg and I are all in here.
How is Mama?

Geraldine goes out

(*Off, as Geraldine*) Much better, Rollo. I'm just going up to change. (*As
Rollo*) You look done in, old girl.

Geraldine comes back in

(*To Mr Beamish*) Just going up to Gerry's room with her.
Mr Beamish (*appalled*) You're what?
Geraldine She's a bit upset, poor poppet. (*She winks at him; then to Reg*)
She says Mama is firing away on all cylinders again, Reg. Down in a mo!

She goes out, kicking the door smartly closed behind her

Mr Beamish looks at Reg. A pause

Mr Beamish I am thunderstruck.
Reg (*numbly*) Yes.
Mr Beamish What am I to *think* of your wife?

Reg (*stifling a groan, hopelessly*) Some sherry?

Mr Beamish (*snapping*) Yes.

Reg pours them a glass each. He takes Mr Beamish his and drinks his own on the way back to the decanter where he refills it

Why your brother?

Reg (*in despair*) Why indeed, Mr Beamish, why why why? Why not my sister?

Mr Beamish What?

Reg Or an aunt or a female cousin or even the matron from my old school. Why my brother?

Mr Beamish (*advancing on him*) Stringer, we are not concerned here with sisters or with matrons.

Reg (*backing away*) You're right of course. After all, the milk is spilt, what's done is done, is there any point in shutting the barn door after a horse of another colour? No.

Mr Beamish Be quiet!

Reg Yes sir. (*He downs his drink*)

Mr Beamish (*pacing about*) Decisions must be made!

Reg Oh God. (*He pursues Mr Beamish*) I do honestly feel that the whole thing can be explained in terms of a very temporary nervous breakdown.

Mr Beamish (*ignoring him*) I must think of my son. My only child marrying into this!

Reg I can quite see that, of course, but I promise you it's chalk and cheese with Billie and her mother. Almost nothing in common. A very stable child. Stolid, phlegmatic, untemperamental——

Mr Beamish (*oblivious of him*) But would he accept my ruling on this? (*A distracted glance at Reg*) This is an impossible situation.

Reg You don't think there's anything to be said in favour of the unconventional mother-in-law?

Mr Beamish (*resuming his pacing*) And he may doubt my word. What evidence have I got? I must keep calm. Marshal the facts. Clarify the issues. Stringer!

Reg (*with sudden energy*) Sir!

Mr Beamish (*pointing à la Kitchener*) A direct personal question!

Reg Fire away!

Mr Beamish I beg your pardon?

Reg (*with suicidal gaiety*) I said fire away. Damn the torpedoes! Full speed ahead!

Mr Beamish (*slightly daunted*) Be that as it may ...

Reg (*beaming*) Absolutely!

Mr Beamish (*ferociously*) Kindly tell me about your wife and your brother.

Reg (*at high speed*) Here is my theory, Mr Beamish, take it or leave it, have it if you will. Or not. Temporarily traumatized by the threat of my redundancy, the humiliations of the dole queue, the house surrounded by howling bank managers, she ... (*He stops. He stares at him*) Did you say my wife *and* my brother?

Mr Beamish (*exasperated*) Yes I did! Your wife and your brother!

Reg (*hardly daring to hope*) Geraldine . . . and . . . Rollo?

Mr Beamish I realize this is painful for you but I must insist that you tell me something about the relationship between Mr Rollo Stringer and your wife.

Reg (*with joyful relief*) Anything!

Mr Beamish What is it?

Reg Anything at all, Mr Beamish. Simply ask.

Mr Beamish (*curtly*) I have asked. What is it?

Reg (*affectionately*) What is what, Mr Beamish?

Mr Beamish (*stentorian*) What is the relationship between your wife and your brother?

Reg Er . . . brother- and sister-in-law, isn't that right?

Mr Beamish I am not speaking of kinship!

Reg Not?

Mr Beamish Not! I am referring to their personal relationship—as, if you'll pardon the expression, man and woman.

Reg (*at sea*) I'm sorry. I don't quite——

Mr Beamish Bite on the bullet, man! Your brother has implied to me in this very room that there is an adulterous connection!

Reg What! She's a liar! (*Hastily*) And so is he!

Mr Beamish You are saying there is no truth in this?

Reg None whatsoever. I swear it.

Mr Beamish A fabrication? A tissue of falsehoods?

Reg Entirely.

Mr Beamish Do you believe this or are you deliberately deceiving yourself?

Reg I know what I know, Mr Beamish.

Mr Beamish Then answer me this! For what reason did your wife and your brother go . . . erm . . . upstairs together?

Reg I—I . . . (*He sighs*) I can only say it simply couldn't be avoided.

Mr Beamish Good God! Do you call yourself a man?

Geraldine appears from the hallway. She is dressed in a long black skirt and a frilly blouse

Reg You're back!

Geraldine (*smiling reproof*) Well I'd hardly stay away tonight of all nights. Mr Beamish, I do apologize. I expect Reg has told you that his mother wasn't quite the thing.

Mr Beamish (*looking toward the hall*) May I ask where Mr Rollo Stringer——

Geraldine Oh sherry! Could I have a teeny glass?

Mesmerized, Reg pours her some. She raises her glass

(*Jubilantly*) Cheers, Reg! Cheers, Mr Beamish! Cheers cheers cheers!

Mr Beamish Mrs Stringer. I would like to know where your——

Reg (*interrupting*) May I say you're looking lovely, Geraldine?

Geraldine (*repressive warmth*) Of course, dear.

Reg You're looking lovely, Geraldine.

Geraldine Thank you, Reginald.

Reg A simple tribute from a simple man. Nothing more.

Geraldine (*a touch of grit*) How nice.

Reg Do you know, Mr Beamish, that Geraldine and I have been married for nearly twenty years and she is still full of surprises for me.

Geraldine (*archly*) Some might say you're a lucky man.

Reg Well, I'm a surprised man.

Mr Beamish (*peremptory*) Stringer, I would like to know if your brother will be rejoining us.

Reg Do you know, I honestly couldn't say. What do you think, dear?

Geraldine (*returning his look steadily*) Rollo? Not at present, I think.

Reg Oh? Why not?

Geraldine (*after a pause*) I believe he wanted to go home and see how Lillian was getting on.

Reg Lillian?

Geraldine (*to Mr Beamish*) Rollo's wife.

Mr Beamish Oh.

Reg Oh! Yes yes! How is Lillian? It's been such an age since we met.

Geraldine Very well. Mr Beamish, your glass is empty.

Reg I know! Why don't Rollo and Lillian dine with us tonight.

Geraldine What?

Reg Do let's ask them. A real family party!

Geraldine (*Medusa*) You know that's impossible.

Reg I don't see why. And Lillian's mad about turkey, you know. I'll just give them a tinkle shall I?

He moves towards the phone. Geraldine intervenes

Geraldine Reg.

Reg Yes, dear?

Geraldine You mustn't be cruel.

Reg (*adrift*) Cruel?

Geraldine (*with charming candour to Mr Beamish*) Rollo's wife, poor Lillian, is mentally unbalanced. It's a terrible pity. She was a brilliant young medical student when they met but for the last twenty years it's just been breakdown after breakdown.

Reg turns away suddenly overcome with laughter

It's tragic for Rollo. Don't you agree, Mr Beamish?

Mr Beamish Well, I—I . . .

Reg (*stifling his laughter, solemnly*) Yes. Poor Rollo. But isn't that all the more reason to ask them round, dear? I'm sure if Lillian could just meet Mr Beamish, he might have a wonderful influence——

Geraldine (*loudly*) Reg, dear, while I'm drinking my sherry, could you go and man the kitchen?

Reg Why not? I might as well man something.

Reg goes

Geraldine Dear Reg, such a quaint sense of humour. More sherry?

Mr Beamish No thank you.

Geraldine (*advancing on him energetically*) Some cashews, then. And do sit down.

He sits suddenly on the edge of a chair. She hands him the nuts

There. Now you look more comfortable.

She sits gracefully and looks at him very benevolently. He avoids her gaze. Then with resolution, he stands up

Mr Beamish Mrs Stringer, I understand that you and your brother-in-law are very close.
Geraldine Oh yes, we're great friends! (*A significant pause*) Well, more than friends really.
Mr Beamish (*giving her a hard look*) I would guess that he is temperamentally very unlike your husband.
Geraldine Ah, so unlike. (*She stretches luxuriantly*) In every way.
Mr Beamish Mrs Stringer, you will forgive me if I do not mince words.
Geraldine (*serious*) I think I know what you're going to say.
Mr Beamish I think you do.
Geraldine You want to tell me you are not a sherry man at all! Let me get you a whisky and soda.
Mr Beamish No. I never touch spirits. Mrs Stringer!
Geraldine Yes, Mr Beamish?
Mr Beamish My son is little more than a child.
Geraldine (*surprised*) Oh is that so? I thought Billie said he was nearly twenty-two.
Mr Beamish A chronological maturity perhaps ... an emotional one, no. The boy must have an atmosphere of steady moral tranquillity and——
Geraldine Oh I see! You refrain from strong drink as an example to your son. How admirable.
Mr Beamish No, that was not the point I—let met put it this way. In my opinion it is the sacred duty of a parent to refrain from any kind of moral laxity.

There is a pause. Then Geraldine faces him courageously

Geraldine Mr Beamish, I don't think you can understand the relief it gives me to hear you say that.
Mr Beamish (*with stern humanity*) Perhaps I can. We are none of us without sin, Mrs Stringer.
Geraldine That's true. Oh so true. Strangely enough, I was saying to Rollo just now as he was carrying the lawn mower upstairs for me——
Mr Beamish Yes it was he that I ... the lawn mower?
Geraldine We have a tiny roof garden. I said to him, "I do pray that Mr Beamish is not a permissive man".
Mr Beamish I——
Geraldine Foolish of me, I can see that now, but knowing that you were a man of power, I feared you might be a man of fashion too.
Mr Beamish I——
Geraldine Sophisticated. Cynical, even.

Mr Beamish No, I——

Geraldine You will think me an old fuddy duddy but I say you cannot go far wrong with the Ten Commandments. Well, nine of them at any rate ... one doesn't really expect murder to crop up. They were preached to me, Mr Beamish, and I preach them to my child. You are right. The parental path is the straight and narrow one. How did you put it on television? Oh yes ... we must light the candles in this naughty world for our children. We are the guardians of their innocence and their purity!

Mr Beamish (*after a pause, moved*) Amen, Mrs Stringer, amen. I see I have been mistaken.

Geraldine You, Mr Beamish?

Mr Beamish To err is human. I too am human.

Geraldine (*warmly*) Surely not.

Mr Beamish (*modestly*) Yes yes. I feel I owe you an apology.

Geraldine (*wide eyed*) An apology?

Mr Beamish Suffice it to say I was sadly misled by your brother-in-law.

Geraldine Rollo? A rough diamond, I'm afraid.

Mr Beamish I have to say I found him boorish and unreliable.

Geraldine (*sadly*) Yes, I can understand that. My bad boy, I sometimes call him. I hope you can make allowances for him, Mr Beamish. Life hasn't been easy for Rollo.

Mr Beamish He's fortunate to have someone as tolerant as yourself for a friend.

Geraldine (*sighing*) I do what I can. I listen to his troubles. I try to guide him ...

Mr Beamish (*gallantly*) Well, may I say Mrs Stringer that if he is your "bad boy" you are his "good fairy".

Geraldine Oh what an enchanting thing to say! You're too kind. You flatter me.

Mr Beamish I never flatter. I am a plain speaking man. I do not hold with pretention. My principles——

Reg comes on dressed in the Jaeger skirt, a blouse and the blue-rinse wig. He carries a bag of golf clubs. He takes out a driver, lines up and executes a drive

Reg (*high and loud*) Fore!

Geraldine and Mr Beamish goggle at him. Reg watches the flight of an imaginary ball

Not one of my best. My fibrositis is troubling me today. (*He puts the club in the bag. Seeing Mr Beamish*) Oh! Mr Beamish! (*He goes to him*) I'm right, aren't I? I'd have known you anywhere after all that Rollo has told me. I am Lillian.

Geraldine Lillian!

Reg Yes, Geraldine, dear?

There is quite a long pause

Geraldine (*shakily*) Shouldn't you be in bed if your fibrositis is bad?

Reg Oh no. Fresh air is the great healer. I am just going out for a round of golf.
Geraldine You can't. It'll be closed.

Reg throws the bag of clubs on the floor and buries his face in his hands

Reg There! I knew it! (*With anguish to Mr Beamish*) They never let me do what I want. Never never never! Is it fair? I ask for so little. I harm no one. Others are allowed a simple frolic, a bit of fun ... (*he shoots a glance at Geraldine*) but not me! Oh no no no no no. (*He rests his head on Mr Beamish's shoulder*) Pity me, Mr Beamish. Pity me.
Mr Beamish Madam, I——
Reg (*to Geraldine*) Oh what a kind and tender-hearted man. The sympathy comes out of him in waves! Geraldine, I would like some whisky.
Geraldine (*snapping*) There isn't any.
Reg Naughty. Mustn't tell fibs. I know where it is and what's more you know that I know. (*He gets the bottle*) Mr Beamish, you'll join me?
Mr Beamish Thank you, no.
Reg Gerry dear? Just a snort?
Geraldine No! (*She essays a smile*) Thank you.
Reg Bottoms up, then!
Geraldine Lillian dear ...
Reg Yes, Gerry?
Geraldine Rollo told me he was going home. He was looking for you as a matter of fact. He'll be dreadfully worried about you.
Reg Rollo never worries.
Geraldine You're wrong.
Reg It's too mean of you, Gerry, you always take his part. Can you deny it? From the very beginning you have taken Rollo's part. (*He takes Mr Beamish cosily by the arm*) Mr Beamish knows what I mean, don't you.
Geraldine (*a note of panic*) Now Lillian ...
Reg (*very bright*) Do you know what I think I'll do, Gerry? I think I'll confide in Mr Beamish.
Geraldine (*a moderate scream*) What?
Reg I know he'll understand. (*He squeezes him*) I feel as if I could tell you anything.
Geraldine (*a bit breathless*) Lillian, please!
Reg Mr Beamish, have you ever been a marriage guidance counsellor?
Mr Beamish No I haven't. What? No.
Reg What a shame. What a sad and terrible shame. And such a waste. Don't you agree, Gerry?
Geraldine I really couldn't——
Reg Mr Beamish is the image of an ideal marriage guidance counsellor. Look at his shoes.
Mr Beamish (*nervously*) My shoes?
Reg Perfect. Reassuring, honourable, compassionate ... with just a hint of irony. You see what I mean don't you, Gerry?
Geraldine No I don't. Lillian go home! Rollo is waiting for you.

Reg You see? Rollo Rollo Rollo. Geraldine is obsessed with Rollo, Mr Beamish, no matter what she says.

Mr Beamish Obsessed?

Geraldine Now Mr Beamish, I told you Lillian is a little——

Reg (*raising his glass*) A toast to Mr Beamish! You have brought something new into our lives, hasn't he, Gerry? It's just like having the Rock of Ages in the house. Life is such a whirl for me, you know, a veritable carousel. Something happens. Then something else happens. I mean the Moving Finger writes so *fast*, don't you find? But in your case I feel . . . do you know what I mean, Geraldine? That in Mr Beamish's case he is writing his autobiography as he goes along. I mean, can you see Mr Beamish singeing a wing in the candle-flame? Never. Can you conceive of him as the ping-pong ball bounced hither and yon on the great breakers of life? No no, he——

Geraldine Now Lillian, you mustn't run on. You're embarrassing Mr Beamish.

Reg Truth never embarrassed anyone, Geraldine, and if it does they ought to be ashamed of themselves!

The phone rings. Reg zestfully picks it up

Hello! This is the Stringer's residence. Who's calling please? (*He holds the phone out to Geraldine*) It's your mother!

Geraldine (*appalled*) Tell her I'll ring her back. I can smell something burning!

Geraldine dashes off to the kitchen

Reg looks helplessly at the phone. Then he thrusts it on Mr Beamish

Reg You speak to her. Do! She's been dying to meet you.

Mr Beamish (*flustered*) Er—Beamish here. Stanley Beamish. . . . What? . . . Ah yes yes yes. How do you do . . . what was that? . . . Who was what? . . . Oh, on the telephone just now? That was——

Reg rushes at him waving his arms wildly. Mr Beamish backs away, terrified

Reg (*a frenzied whisper*) No no no! Don't tell her! She mustn't know I'm here!

Mr Beamish (*eyes fixed on Reg, into the phone*) I don't know. I don't know who it was. . . . What? . . . I said no. No idea. No idea at all. . . . Madam, are you doubting my word? (*After a pause*) Of course. Certainly. Not at all. Good-night.

He hangs up. Reg advances on him and he backs away clutching the phone to his breast

Reg Oh Mr Beamish, how can I thank you? You must have thought I was mad!

Mr Beamish No no. Oh no. No.

Reg You are simply a knight in shining armour.

Mr Beamish A what?

Reg How many men would have sacrificed truth on the altar of chivalry? How often is a . . . (*He breaks off*) Did you want to make a phone call?

Mr Beamish (*looking at the phone*) Oh. No.

Reg (*taking it from him*) Only a man of honour, integrity and charity would perjure himself in a compassionate cause, am I right?

Mr Beamish (*modestly*) Oh well, I . . .

Reg I am. I know I am. Geraldine's mother doesn't understand me, Mr Beamish. She wants to have me certified. But I am a harmless case! Ask anyone. She mustn't know I was here tonight. She thinks I'm in a nursing home in Felixstowe.

Mr Beamish Felixstowe?

Reg And I would be, Mr Beamish, I would be! I would put myself in their hands this instant but I don't believe in psychiatrists.

Mr Beamish Very sensible of you. I don't myself.

Reg You don't? How wonderful. (*Confiding*) Some people see them everywhere. Mr Beamish, will you promise me never never to tell Geraldine's mother that you met me?

Mr Beamish Yes I do. I promise.

Reg (*emotional*) I am safe in the bright circle of your goodness.

Geraldine comes in from the kitchen with swift resolve

Geraldine (*taking Reg by the arm*) Lillian, it's time for your tablets.

Reg Oh Gerry, do you know that the minute I clapped eyes on Mr Beamish I thought—here is a man of enlightenment. Honourable, just, wise and strong . . . a higher being.

Mr Beamish (*very pleased*) Oh now . . .

Geraldine (*pulling Reg towards the hall*) Come along. You know what the doctor said. And then we'll pop you straight home to bed and——

There is the sound of the front door. They freeze

Billie (*off*) We're back!

Geraldine rushes Reg towards the kitchen

Geraldine They're in the kitchen! Your tablets!

Reg and Geraldine go. Billie and Bunny come in from the hall. Geraldine comes back from the kitchen

(*Vivaciously*) Billie dear! Here's Mr Beamish.

Billie How do you do.

Mr Beamish How do you do, Miss Stringer.

Bunny (*peering in the direction of his voice*) Dad?

Mr Beamish (*peering back*) Hello, my boy.

Billie Bunny, this is my mother. Mother, this is Bun.

Bunny moves towards Geraldine, hand outstretched. He trips over and ricochets off furniture in his progress and finally achieves her hand

Bunny How do you do.

Geraldine How do you do.

Billie (*admiringly*) Bunny's trying to discipline himself to do without his glasses. Where's Daddy by the way?

Geraldine Here any moment, dear. (*To Bunny*) How terribly terribly interesting. Do tell me about it.

Bunny (*pleased*) Oh. Uh . . . well . . . it's my theory that most of us like to . . . um . . . use our minor disabilities as a kind of . . . um . . . refuge. I mean . . . what I mean is it's a way of having to be . . . well not having to be, rather . . . uh . . . responsible for ourselves . . . or no, for our actions. Well both really . . . I haven't explained that very well.

Geraldine Oh you have. (*A glance at the kitchen*) It's simply fascinating! Do tell me more.

Bunny Well in my own case of course I'm in what you might call a conflict with my . . . um . . . genetic heritage. I've inherited poor eyesight from a long line of myopic ancestors . . .

Mr Beamish Poppycock. The eyesight in our family has always been excellent. I myself have twenty-twenty vision.

Billie But Mr Beamish . . . you're wearing glasses.

Mr Beamish These are reading glasses.

There is a sound from the kitchen

(*To Geraldine*) Do you think your sister-in-law is all right?

Billie Sister-in-law?

Mr Beamish Your Aunt Lillian.

Geraldine Oh God. I mean, please don't worry, Mr Beamish. I'm sure everything's——

Mr Beamish (*heading for the kitchen*) She may require assistance.

Geraldine tries to get there first

Let me handle this, Mrs Stringer. I think she trusts me.

Mr Beamish goes out to the kitchen

Billie (*bewildered*) Who's in the kitchen?

Geraldine (*categorically*) Nobody.

Billie Well what's wrong with Mr Beamish then? Who trusts him? What does he mean? Bunny, is your father potty?

Bunny Yes, but I've never known him to have hallucinations.

Mr Beamish (*off*) No no, don't run away. I'm not going to hurt you.

Geraldine (*tremulously*) I think I should just go and . . .

Before she can move Mr Beamish comes out leading Reg who stands with his eyes cast down

Mr Beamish Here we are! All friends here, dear lady. (*Aside to Geraldine*) I've locked the back door. (*He holds up the key and pockets it*)

Billie My . . . Aunt . . . Lillian?

Geraldine (*with lunatic buoyancy*) Yes isn't it a surprise to see her tonight. She just popped in!

Billie strides with purposeful menace towards Reg who dodges her

Reg I've had the most wonderful idea, Mr Beamish. I'm going to write you a little book called *How To Have Fun After Redundancy*. Good title? Or am I just being silly?

Mr Beamish Not at all. Excellent title. May I introduce my son? This is Mrs Lillian Stringer, Bun. Our Mr Stringer's brother's wife.

Billie Brother? Mother!

Geraldine (*dodging her*) Canapés! I forgot the canapés!

Geraldine belts out to the kitchen

Billie turns to Reg who gets behind Bunny

Reg So you're Bunny. How nice. How terribly nice. You don't look a bit like your father, do you, but then why should you? No reason in the world. (*As Billie comes round the other side at him, he dodges again*) I always think we're all like some mysterious crossword puzzle of Mother Nature's, don't you?

Billie starts to speak. He rushes on

And I'm sure you're like your father in other ways. Such a kind, generous sympathetic man.

Mr Beamish (*pleased*) No no.

Reg (*aggressively*) Yes yes! Yes yes yes! Where are my clubs?

Bunny Clubs?

Mr Beamish (*therapeutically*) Mrs Stringer is a great golfer.

Reg Oh my goodness yes. Simply love it. (*Again getting away from Billie*) Mad about it! Mad! *Vive le sport! Absolument*, don't you know. Oh here we are. Hello little clubs, I've found you. (*Anxiously*) But have I lost my balls?

Geraldine has come in with plates of canapés

Gerry, I think I've lost my——

Billie (*loudly*) Mother!

Geraldine (*evading her*) Canapé, Mr Beamish? Do try one of my grilled husbands.

Mr Beamish (*astonished*) Husbands?

Geraldine Mushrooms! Mushrooms! How silly I am.

Billie (*cornering her*) Mother . . .

Geraldine Yes, dear?

Billie What has happened to my father?

Geraldine (*wonderfully calm*) Called away briefly, Billie. (*She fixes Reg with a terrible smile*) But he'll be back any moment.

Billie (*desperately*) Are you sure?

Geraldine Positive. (*After a pause. Inspiration*) As a matter of fact, Aunt Lillian wants to be getting home. Could you take her?

Billie (*promptly*) I'll get the car. (*She starts out*)

Reg (*springing over to Bunny and taking his arm*) Bunny will come along for the drive, won't you, Bunny? I'd adore you to see my little home.

Bunny Oh. Right. Thanks very much.

Reg (*taking Mr Beamish's arm too*) And you'll come too, won't you, Mr Beamish?

Mr Beamish Of course, if you would like me to.

Reg (*jumping for joy*) I would I would I would! Well, we're all ready to go!

Geraldine (*after a pause; hideous good humour*) Do you know what I think? I think it's too silly for you to go home now when dinner's nearly ready. Stay Lillian, do.

Reg Oh Gerry, you don't want poor little me.

Geraldine (*snapping*) Yes I do.

Reg (*crossing to her*) I shouldn't be tempted. I know I shouldn't but it's so sweet of you, Gerry. I'd love to stay!

He kisses her on the cheek. Billie hurls a plate of canapés to the floor. Black-out

CURTAIN

ACT II

The same. Later that evening

Music

The Lights come up. There are sounds of the dinner party off stage

Geraldine and Billie come in carrying the coffee tray, etc.

Billie What's happened to him?
Geraldine What?
Billie What's happened to Daddy?
Geraldine I'm as baffled by all this as you are, Billie.
Billie But what started it? What triggered it off?
Geraldine I have absolutely no idea.
Billie And what's all this "Uncle Rollo"?
Geraldine Nothing. A figment. An hallucination. Nothing at all.

A burst of merriment from off stage, Reg's Lillian laugh loudest

Billie Oh what are we going to do? All through supper I kept thinking "any
second now, any second now".
Geraldine Exactly! How he thought he could get away with——
Billie I've taken Bun's glasses out of his jacket pocket. (*She goes and puts
them behind something*) It's Mr Beamish I'm worried about. If he finds out
he'll never let Bunny marry me! He'll just ... (*She breaks off*) Oh God,
how can I be so selfish! Poor Daddy!
Geraldine Poor! What do you mean, poor?
Billie This breakdown.
Geraldine He is not having a breakdown!
Billie But Mother, what else could it be? Nobody in their right mind would
dress up like the opposite sex when the boss was coming to dinner. I mean
they wouldn't, would they?
Geraldine Well ... no ... I ...
Billie You're worried it might be repressed homosexuality aren't you?
Geraldine What!
Billie Well don't. Honestly. I've read a lot about this kind of thing. The
mid-life crisis. Male menopause. The symptoms don't mean anything in
themselves. I just wish it hadn't happened tonight. (*With resolve*) Listen
Mother, I'll go and tell him you want to speak to him for a minute. I can
keep the others talking at table.
Geraldine Oh Billie, he won't listen to me.
Billie Just be very firm and very gentle. Tell him we understand and we're

not angry, we're only worried about him and he's got to go to bed and take a sleeping pill and tomorrow we'll call a psychiatrist.

Billie goes

(*Off*) Aunt Lillian . . .

Geraldine paces angrily about

Reg comes through the kitchen door. He calls back through it

Reg Back in a jiffy. (*Then to Geraldine*) All right, don't say it. I'll go and change.

Geraldine I see. Just like that.

Reg What?

Geraldine You've had your fun, you've completely ruined the evening, you've victimized your wife and daughter and now it's just "I'll go and change". Charming!

Reg Wait a minute.

Geraldine It's revenge, isn't it?

Reg It's what?

Geraldine Just because you subscribe to the women-are-brutes school of thought——

Reg I don't.

Geraldine Yes you do. You told me I was a bully. And what about my mother?

Reg That's different. I've never thought of your mother as a woman.

Geraldine Oh ha ha. And what's so unfair is Billie thinks you're in a mid-life crisis.

Reg (*delighted*) She does? Oh good. She's not angry with me then?

Geraldine No, but I am. And she ought to be. Tonight of all nights!

Reg I don't believe this!

Geraldine How could you be so selfish?

Reg Listen, Gerry, you started all this.

Geraldine Yes but I wasn't going to go on and on with it. Mine was just a little lark, not a major production number. It's so typical of you. You steal my idea and have all the fun and I get stuck with the cover-ups and the——

Reg Right. I won't change.

Geraldine What?

Reg I'll stay.

Geraldine (*in a rage*) Reg! Listen to me——

Bunny comes in

Bunny (*hearing this and stopping dead*) Reg?

Reg and Geraldine freeze. Then Reg breaks into fluent Lillian

Reg Of course I'm listening, Gerry dear. Calm down. There there. You're not to be upset. (*To Bunny*) Gerry's so upset about Reg. (*To her*) He'll be perfectly all right, I promise. It's probably only a migraine.

Geraldine Do you really think so, Lillian?

Bunny (*peering round*) I thought I heard a man's voice.

Geraldine Lillian's such a comfort to me, Bun. I've been so frightened it might be a brain tumour or something. Reg has been a mass of nerves lately and much more timid than usual. Afraid of the dark, terrified of the milkman ... and bicycles!

Bunny He's afraid of bicycles?

Geraldine Yes. Isn't it lucky we don't live in Holland?

Reg Dear girl, always exaggerating ...

Bunny Aunt Lillian—you're sure you don't mind if I call you Aunt Lillian ...?

Reg I love it! (*A complacent glance at Geraldine*)

Bunny Billie's just told me you're about to leave.

Reg No no.

Geraldine Yes yes. Lillian felt she must run along.

Bunny I wish you wouldn't go.

Geraldine She must she must she must! (*Steering Reg out*) Off we go.

Bunny goes over to the kitchen door and listens

Reg (*stopping*) Oh I've been such a juggins. I forgot to bring a coat with me. Gerry, would you be a sweetheart and lend me a woolly? Sorry to be such a bother.

Geraldine (*after a pause*) I'll go and get one.

Geraldine goes

Bunny (*coming back*) My father's giving Billie his Beamish Books Centenary speech. The Centenary isn't for eleven years but he likes to practise. Aunt Lillian, do you think you could give me some advice?

Reg I could try.

Bunny It's about Billie. Let me start by saying that I'm in love with Billie. As far as I'm concerned it's just like Tristan and—and ...

Reg (*enthusiastically*) Isolde!

Bunny (*unnerved*) Sorry?

Reg Isolde. Tristan and Isolde.

Bunny Right! Those are the ones. She's a wonderful girl. Billie, I mean. Woman. She's a wonderful woman. They don't like being called girl. Though as a matter of fact Billie doesn't mind. Which is part of the problem. She's got some quite old-fashioned ideas and ... oh.

Geraldine comes in with a cardigan

Geraldine Here you are, Lillian.

Reg Oh I don't want to wear that old thing. I know! The white angora your mother knitted you. Let me borrow that.

Geraldine You can't.

Reg Why?

Geraldine Because I don't know where it is.

Reg Oh please find it, Gerry. Please!

Geraldine (*through clenched teeth*) Will you put this on.

Reg (*building to a tantrum*) No! I don't want to! I won't go home unless I can wear the white angora!

Geraldine (*after a pause; very calm*) I'll see if I can find it.

Geraldine goes, slamming the door behind her

Reg Now Bunny, this problem . . .

Bunny Well the thing is, Aunt Lillian, I'm not sure that Billie has real faith in our love for each other. I mean, that's what's going to keep us together, not saying some words in front of a vicar. All right, so her parents are still together even though they're bored with each other and the whole thing seems a bit pointless but what I say——

Reg Bored with each other?

Bunny So she says.

Reg Pointless?

Bunny Yes. Sad, isn't it? You know what I think, Aunt Lillian? I think somebody should write a book for my father's firm called *How To Say I Do To Life!*

Reg Yes, perhaps they should.

Bunny I mean if you asked me what life was all about I'd say it's about chance and risk and hazard and . . . and surprises! After all, isn't the whole of evolution just a series of surprises?

Reg Ye-es . . . I suppose you could say that. (*He straightens his wig*)

Bunny I'm going to tell Billie tonight.

Reg Tell her what?

Bunny That it's wrong for us to get engaged or married or any of that. We should simply decide that we want to live with each other forever and——

Reg Bunny . . .

Bunny Yes?

Reg I don't know that I'd tell her all that tonight . . .

Bunny But I have to. It's tonight she wants to tell everybody we're engaged.

Geraldine comes on with a white cardigan

Geraldine Here it is.

Mr Beamish and Billie come on from the kitchen

Billie It's an inspiring story, Mr Beamish. (*She sees Reg*) Mother!

Geraldine Oh there you are. Lillian's just leaving.

Billie Goodbye, Aunt Lillian.

Mr Beamish I'm sorry to hear that. What a pretty jacket.

Reg Isn't it stunning? It belongs to Gerry and it's Rollo's favourite. He simply adores you in this sweater, doesn't he, Gerry? He loves stroking it . . . the feel of it. (*Stroking himself very sensuously*) Try it, Mr Beamish.

Mr Beamish backs away and glares at Geraldine

Geraldine Come along now, Lillian. Don't be silly.

Reg (*eluding her; going to Bunny*) Do you like it? It's angora. Bunny! Just like you. Bunny! (*He peals with laughter*) Oh I'm having such a good time.

(*He claps his hands*) Do you know, I've changed my mind! I'll wait for Rollo to come and collect me.

Geraldine He is not coming!

Reg Oh Gerry, Gerry, will you never learn to say "I do" to life? (*To Mr Beamish*) Rollo can never stay away from Gerry for long.

Mr Beamish What's that?

Reg Oh yes, he's here day and night, night and day I promise you. (*Sudden tears*) Oh Rollo Rollo, what did I do wrong? Why is she your Lorelei and not me? Why? Why? Why?

He bursts into sobs and throws himself on to the sofa

Mr Beamish Mrs Stringer! You told me that you and——

Geraldine Mr Beamish, why don't you and Bunny help yourselves to coffee. Billie and I will look after her. (*To Reg*) Poor sweetheart. Don't cry. We're here. (*Bundling him out, a ferocious whisper*) Get out! Get out!

Billie It'll be all right, Aunt Lillian. What you need is a nice rest.

Billie and Geraldine get Reg out

Mr Beamish (*to Bunny*) Have you bought a ring?

Bunny A what?

Mr Beamish A ring, a ring, an engagement ring, have you bought one?

Bunny Oh. (*Bravely*) No. I'm not going to.

Mr Beamish What?

Bunny I decided tonight.

Mr Beamish (*with dawning hope*) Not going to get engaged?

Bunny (*not looking at him*) No. Or married.

Mr Beamish (*emotionally*) I can't believe my ears.

Bunny I'm sorry, Dad. I realize your generation——

Mr Beamish (*advancing on him*) Sorry, my boy? Sorry?

Bunny (*backing away*) Dad, please. I know it's a shock for you——

Reg (*off stage, as Lillian*) I don't want to go and lie down. I won't! I won't!

Mr Beamish (*going to the door; opening it*) Can I be of assistance?

Geraldine, Billie and Reg are struggling in the doorway

Geraldine No, thanks so much, Mr Beamish. Everything's under control.

Geraldine shuts the door again

Mr Beamish Now, Bun ...

Bunny Don't try and change my mind, Dad. I know how you feel but I've made my decision and I'm sticking to it!

Mr Beamish And I will back you, Bun! Every inch of the way!

Bunny (*astounded*) You will? You? You mean you think I'm right?

Mr Beamish Completely and entirely and altogether right. It will be a blow of course, but convention and manners must take second place here.

Bunny Convention and ... Dad! I can't believe this is you talking. It's incredible! You're on my side! I would have sworn on a stack of Bibles that you——

Mr Beamish You are my only son, Bun. If there is a side to be on, it is yours, lad. She's a charming girl——
Bunny Oh she is. (*Troubled*) She's going to be upset about this.
Mr Beamish You mean you haven't told her?
Bunny Well not yet. I really only decided——

The doorbell rings

Reg (*off, as Lillian, from upstairs*) I'll get it!

His footsteps are heard running down the stairs. The door opens. He screams. He comes on running fast, and disappears into the kitchen. He is followed by Mrs Carmichael who stands and watches him run

Geraldine and Billie come on

Mrs Carmichael Geraldine! Who was that?
Geraldine Nobody at all, Mother, no-one of any——
Mrs Carmichael Billie, who was that person?
Billie Granny! How wonderful that you could come after all. Look, Bunny, it's my grandmother! Here she is! I've told Bunny so much about you, haven't I, Bunny?
Mrs Carmichael I don't understand. What is all the mystery? Why am I not to be told who that was?
Bunny (*helpfully*) It was only Aunt——
Mr Beamish (*loudly*) Bun! (*He fixes Mrs Carmichael with a look*) That was a neighbour. A Mrs Blick. She came to borrow a cup of sugar.

The others stare at him

Geraldine (*hushed awe*) Mr Beamish!
Bunny (*flabbergasted*) Dad, what do you——?
Mr Beamish (*to him*) Shush! (*Going to Mrs Carmichael*) I think you must be Mrs Carmichael. We met earlier this evening. Telephonically. Beamish. Stanley Beamish.
Mrs Carmichael (*shaking hands, stunned*) How do you do. But why did she run away from me? She screamed. She seemed terrified. I've never met the woman in my life.
Mr Beamish She is insane. May I say that it's difficult for me to believe that you and Mrs Stringer can be mother and daughter. Sisters!
Mrs Carmichael (*simpering*) Oh heavens.
Bunny (*surfacing again*) Dad, I still don't see why you——
Mr Beamish A word with you, my boy. (*To the others*) Will you excuse us? (*He takes him aside*)
Billie Coffee, Granny? Have some coffee.
Geraldine Yes do, Mother. Let me get it.
Mrs Carmichael Thank you, dear. But I can't understand how you could allow that——

Geraldine and Billie manage to overwhelm Mrs Carmichael with attention and chat

Mr Beamish (*to Bunny*) Mrs Carmichael mustn't know that Aunt Lillian was here tonight. She wants to have her certified as a dangerous lunatic.

Bunny God, that's terrible. Right. I'm with you, Dad.

Mrs Carmichael But shouldn't someone get this person out of the kitchen and send her home?

Geraldine Oh she'll have gone out the back door by now.

Mr Beamish Bound to have done . . . oh. (*He takes the back-door key out of his pocket*)

Geraldine (*seeing it*) Oh.

Mrs Carmichael Is something wrong?

Mr Beamish No no, I—I haven't introduced my son. Shake hands with Mrs Carmichael, Bun.

Mrs Carmichael How do you do.

As she and Bunny shake hands, Mr Beamish and Geraldine move cautiously towards each other

Mrs Carmichael Geraldine!

Geraldine stops dead

Isn't he the image of his father!

Geraldine Yes, he certainly is.

Again, she and Mr Beamish make for each other

Mrs Carmichael Do sit down, Mr Beamish.

Mr Beamish Ah. Yes. Thank you. (*He sits*)

Geraldine (*sidling over to sit beside him*) Mr Beamish enjoyed your green olive and chestnut stuffing very much, didn't you Mr Beamish?

Mr Beamish Magnificent.

Geraldine (*sitting*) My mother is a wonderful, wonderful cook.

Mr Beamish I'm sure of it. (*He slips her the key*)

Geraldine (*sotto voce*) Thanks so much. (*She gets up and aims for the kitchen*)

Mrs Carmichael Geraldine . . . all this talk of cooking. Do you know, I am ravenous. Nothing on the train, of course. You won't mind if I go and cut myself a little turkey sandwich.

Geraldine (*forestalling her*) I'll get it for you, Mother.

As she reaches the kitchen door it opens

Reg comes in with a tea-towel tied over the lower part of his face and carrying a cup of sugar

Reg makes for the hall, waving and bowing in a sort of general way and moving fairly swiftly. They all watch silently. Then Mrs Carmichael steps forward to block his way

Mrs Carmichael One moment, Mrs Black.

Reg Blick! Blick! Thanks so much for the sugar. Lovely to meet you. Goodbye.

Mrs Carmichael That voice! I recognize that voice!

Reg freezes and shuts his eyes

Billie (*quaveringly*) Ohhhhh . . .
Geraldine (*hopelessly*) You're imagining things, Mother.
Mrs Carmichael I am not. (*She points at Reg*) It was you!
Reg No! No it wasn't! No!
Mrs Carmichael Yes! On the telephone more than two hours ago! You have obviously been here the whole evening. Mrs Blick! I'm ashamed of you!

Everyone exchanges glances of amazed relief

And why have you got that tea-towel over your face?
Reg (*making for the door*) It's a yashmak. I'm a recent convert to Islam. Cheeribye all!
Mrs Carmichael (*stopping him*) Islam? Why? Explain yourself.
Geraldine Good-night, Mrs Blick, you'd better be getting home. (*Aside*) Mother, she's a bit . . .
Mrs Carmichael I'm sorry but to me that is no excuse for bad behaviour. It's my opinion that all this talk of mental illness is simply socialistic self-indulgence. We must pull ourselves together, Mrs Blick, not fall back on our nerves. It's like all this whining about unemployment. If people really wanted to work, they'd work. I'm sure you agree with me there, Mr Beamish.
Mr Beamish Well, yes. Yes I do of course, but——
Mrs Carmichael I blame the unions. And I blame the woman's movement. I was speaking on the topic only tonight. If women must move, let them move backwards, I said. Back! Back! Back to your larders, back to your sewing baskets, back to your bread and butter puddings, to your . . . (*She breaks off*) Mrs Blick! That is my daughter's angora cardigan! Take it off at once!

She yanks at the sweater and catches the tea-towel which comes off. She screams. A terrible pause

(*Breathless with horror*) What does this mean? Geraldine! What has happened to Reginald?
Geraldine (*top speed*) Reg wasn't very well this evening, Mother. He was running a little temperature. He's gone to lie down, take an aspirin, put his feet up . . . surely you remember Aunt Lillian!
Mrs Carmichael (*an appalled hiss*) Have you taken leave of your senses? (*She advances on Reg who backs away*) I demand to know what all this——
Mr Beamish (*commandingly*) Mrs Carmichael!

She turns

I'm afraid I must take the blame for this.

Everyone stares at him

Mrs Carmichael (*aghast*) You?
Mr Beamish Yes. *Mea culpa*, I have to say it. I knew of your prejudice against Aunt Lillian . . .

Mrs Carmichael My ... ?

Mr Beamish Presumptuous of me, perhaps. I was trying to protect her.

Reg (*running to him*) Oh Mr Beamish!

Mr Beamish There there. In the past I'll confess that I too have had limited patience with madness. But tonight I think I have begun to see the other fellow's point of view.

Mrs Carmichael The ... other ... fellow?

Mr Beamish Aunt Lillian has touched my heart, Mrs Carmichael. A lost creature, yes. All at sixes and sevens it's true. But there is a quite extraordinary precipience. Aunt Lillian has seen through me.

Mrs Carmichael Seen through *you*?

Mr Beamish (*nodding gravely*) Yes. Behind my somewhat stern façade, there is a man of compassion. A Man Who Cares. She has found that man.

Reg starts to laugh uncontrollably and hides his face in his hands

Don't cry, Aunt Lillian. Be brave. Now do you know what I want you to do? I want you and Mrs Carmichael to shake hands and be friends. (*He steers Reg over to her*) Will you do that, Mrs Carmichael?

Mrs Carmichael numbly shakes hands with Reg

(*Solemnly*) Thank you.

Reg Oh I'm so thrilled that we're going to be chums. Do you play golf?

Mrs Carmichael (*stonily*) No.

Reg Never mind, I'll teach you. Now you must call me Lily and I'll call you Aggie.

Mrs Carmichael My name is Agatha. No-one has ever called me Aggie.

Reg Oh goody, then I'll be the first.

Mrs Carmichael (*still looking at Reg*) Geraldine, a word with you please.

Geraldine Not now, Mother. I'm just going to get everyone a liqueur.

Reg Oh I'll do that, Gerry. You have your little chat with Aggie. Billie will help me.

He shepherds the fuming Geraldine over to her mother. He and Billie take the others upstage to organize the liqueurs

Mrs Carmichael How in God's name could you allow him to do this!

Geraldine Mother, he's having a nervous breakdown.

Mrs Carmichael Nonsense! He is simply depraved and degenerate! Now. Here is the plan. You must get Mr Beamish and his son to leave as soon as possible. And you must tell Mr Beamish that Billie is adopted.

Geraldine Adopted! Why?

Mrs Carmichael If all this ever comes out he will naturally fear the blood is tainted. Then there's the question of getting rid of Reginald ... and I mean for good.

Geraldine Perhaps you should hire a hit man.

Mrs Carmichael Don't be ridiculous, Geraldine. I am not a rich woman, as you know. You will start divorce proceedings first thing Monday morning.

Geraldine I won't.

Mrs Carmichael You will do as I say! And that's final.

Reg (*bringing them glasses*) Brandy for the ladies?

Bunny I'd like to propose a toast.

Reg Lovely!

Bunny To my father. I feel I've never known him until tonight. (*He raises his glass*) Dad.

All Mr Beamish.

Mr Beamish (*beaming*) Well well. I'm very touched.

Mrs Carmichael And to round off the evening, a toast to the happy couple.

Billie (*pleased*) Oh Granny . . .

Bunny (*as they all start the toast*) There's something I'd like to say about that. To Billie.

Mr Beamish My boy, is this the moment?

Billie What is it, Bun?

Reg Heavens! How can we all be so thoughtless! Billie dear, take your grandmother out to the kitchen and get her a nice turkey sandwich. She's as hungry as a wild boar, aren't you, Aggie?

Mrs Carmichael makes a menacing move toward him. Billie intervenes

Billie Yes. You come with me, Granny. (*She leads her off. Low*) I'll explain everything to you. I know you'll understand.

Mrs Carmichael (*eyes closed*) I will not.

Billie and Mrs Carmichael go to the kitchen

Reg Well! What a lovely evening. I do congratulate you, Gerry. Wonderful food, wonderful company . . . How do you do it? I don't know when I've had so much fun.

Geraldine (*fanged*) Don't you?

Reg Cross my heart. Such a pity Rollo never came back. We miss him, don't we, Gerry? Now. Do you know what I'm going to do? I'm going to skip upstairs and see if Reg is feeling better. I'm sure I can persuade him to come down and join us.

He starts out but Geraldine cuts him off

Geraldine No don't you bother, Lillian, I'll go.

Mr Beamish takes Bunny aside to speak to him

Reg (*low*) You don't understand. I'm going to change back.

Geraldine No you're not. You've made your bed. Now have fun on it. I'm going and I'm not coming back.

Reg (*in his own voice, loud*) No!

Mr Beamish and Bunny look over, startled

(*Lillian's voice*) You must let me go, Gerry. I insist! I insist!

Geraldine (*leading Reg forcibly to a chair*) Goodness Lillian, there's no need for you to go dashing about running errands. So bad for your fibrositis.

You just sit down and relax and enjoy yourself. (*To Mr Beamish*) You'll excuse me?

She smiles all round and goes

Reg leaps up to follow her

Mr Beamish Aunt Lillian——
Reg Back in a tick.
Mr Beamish (*taking his arm*) Spare us a moment, won't you?
Reg (*trying to get loose*) I think Gerry——
Mr Beamish Bun has just told me he's confided in you.
Reg Oh yes yes yes! The dear boy! Now if you'll just——
Mr Beamish He is rejecting marriage categorically.
Reg Bunny! You didn't tell your father!
Mr Beamish He did—and his father stands by him and rejects it too.
Reg (*stunned*) You do?
Mr Beamish I do.
Bunny (*admiringly*) Would you ever have guessed it, Aunt Lillian?
Reg (*mouth open, shaking his head*) I never would!
Mr Beamish A wise and courageous decision to my mind. But I'm sure you'll agree it's something he should discuss in private with your niece.
Reg My what? Oh. Billie.

Billie comes in unnoticed and hears the following exchange

Bunny The point is I already know exactly how she's going to react. She's got this obsession with bridesmaids and wedding bouquets and——
Mr Beamish Bun. That is rather a callous way to talk when a young girl's feelings—oh . . . Miss Stringer.
Billie (*businesslike*) Bunny, would you go and put the hood up on the car? It's started to rain. Aunt Lillian, will you go with him and show him how it works please.
Reg Don't you move, Bunny. (*Dashing out*) I can manage it all by myself.

Reg goes

Bunny (*to the others*) She's fantastic! (*He calls*) Wait for me, Aunt Lillian.

Bunny goes

Billie Mr Beamish, I need your advice.
Mr Beamish (*instant Solomon*) Certainly. How can I help?
Bunny (*off*) Why are you going upstairs, Aunt Lillian?
Reg (*off*) Just fetching an umbrella, dear.
Bunny (*off*) But there's one right here in the hall. Look. Aren't you coming?
Reg (*off, defeated*) I'm coming.
Billie (*as the front door closes*) It's about Bunny.
Mr Beamish Ah. Well, in my opinion, you and he must——
Billie I know what he wants to say to me.
Mr Beamish You do?
Billie (*sighing*) Oh yes.

Mr Beamish (*at a loss*) Well I can only say that I'm extremely sorry.

Billie Poor Granny. I really think it would break her heart.

Mr Beamish *Her* heart?

Billie Oh it's important to me too, I don't mind admitting it. But the thing is, it's just what my parents did. Granny never forgave them.

Mr Beamish I'm not sure I follow. Your parents did what?

Billie Well they didn't, that's the point. They wouldn't.

Mr Beamish Wouldn't what?

Billie But in those days the whole attitude to marriage was different, wasn't it.

Mr Beamish Attitude to marriage?

Billie You know. The swinging sixties and everything. I mean they just couldn't be bothered.

Mr Beamish Miss Stringer! Are you telling me that your mother and father are not——

Billie But Granny and I believe in the traditional values. And I know you do too, Mr Beamish.

Mr Beamish But—but . . . that makes you a——

Billie And besides, we've picked out the dress. You can't wear a wedding dress in a registry office.

Mr Beamish Registry——

Billie It would look silly.

Mr Beamish Oh. Oh I see. Your parents were married in a registry office.

Billie That's right. Like Bunny wants for him and me. Oh Mr Beamish, couldn't you persuade him? Granny and I have planned everything. Four bridesmaids . . . and a page boy . . . Granny's butcher's son . . .

Mr Beamish Miss Stringer, come and sit down. I find myself in a most awkward position.

Billie You mean you won't persuade him? Oh I was so sure you'd be on my side.

Mr Beamish I mustn't let you go on cherishing false hopes.

Billie But don't you think a church wedding is important?

Mr Beamish Yes I do.

Billie Then why won't you persuade him?

Mr Beamish You must be brave, Miss Stringer.

Billie Brave?

Mr Beamish Bun has told me tonight that he is not ready to make this commitment.

Billie (*with dread*) What do you mean . . . commitment?

Mr Beamish To the engagement. To the marriage. He has changed his mind.

Billie (*leaping up*) What? Do you mean he wants to break the whole thing off? Bunny's jilting me?

The sound of the front door opening and closing

Bunny and Reg come in from the front hall. Bunny is nursing a finger

Bunny It's really OK, Aunt Lillian. It was my own stupid fault.

Billie Bunny! Is it true?

Bunny Well I had my hand right under the bracket when——
Billie Your father says you don't want to marry me!
Bunny Dad! You told her!
Billie (*wailing*) Then it is true! Granny!

Mrs Carmichael comes in from the kitchen

Mrs Carmichael Billie! What is it? What's wrong?
Billie (*sobbing*) Oh Granny . . .
Bunny (*to Mr Beamish*) But why? You were making such a big thing about how I should be the one to——
Reg Bunny, tell Billie you don't mean that you——
Mrs Carmichael What have you done to upset Billie?

They are all shouting at once

Geraldine comes in as Rollo

Geraldine What's all the racket?

Mrs Carmichael screams and falls into a chair

Reg Rollo! You've come back!
Geraldine That's right, my little chickadee.
Mrs Carmichael (*shrieking again*) I can't bear it! It's a nightmare!
Billie (*murderously calm*) It's all right, Granny. It's only Uncle Rollo.
Geraldine That's it. What ho, Mrs C. Not often we see you here, eh? Only every day, ha ha ha.
Mr Beamish (*coldly*) Where is your sister-in-law?
Geraldine (*winking*) Lying down. (*She slaps him on the back*) How was the turkey, Stanley old man? Hope they didn't give you that godawful green olive stuffing.

Sound of rage from Mrs Carmichael

And this must be Bun the son.

They shake hands

We haven't met. Lillian's better half ha ha ha. (*She turns ferociously on Reg*) And what the devil do you think you're doing in Gerry's angora? You're a kleptomaniac now on top of everything else? Take it off!

She advances threateningly on Reg who screams

Mr Beamish Sir, you are a bully and a cad!
Geraldine No man calls me cad, Beamish. Choose your weapons!
Reg (*rushing to shield Mr Beamish*) Don't touch him!
Geraldine Out of my way, Lillian!
Reg Bun! Stop him!

Bunny gets hold of Geraldine and holds her back

Mr Beamish is what you'll never be, Rollo. A real man . . . a wonderful chivalrous man!
Geraldine I suppose you're in love with him.

Reg I worship him!

Geraldine I'll kill him!

Reg You'll have to kill me first!

Mrs Carmichael (*leaping to her feet in blind rage*) Stop this at once! I will not allow you to——

Reg Yes, Aggie dear?

Geraldine You've got a suggestion, Mrs C?

Mrs Carmichael Yes I have! (*She takes a deep breath, then looks from Reg and Geraldine to Mr Beamish and back again*) No. (*She sits down*)

Billie (*in cold rage*) It's Islington all over again, isn't it!

Mr Beamish Islington, Miss Stringer?

Billie Yes! I said Islington, yes! Do you remember it *Uncle* Rollo and *Aunt* Lillian? Well? Do you?

Bunny (*putting his arm round her*) Calm down, Billie.

Billie Don't touch me. I hate you!

Bunny Hate me!

Mrs Carmichael (*bounding over*) She doesn't mean that.

Billie Be quiet, Granny!

Mrs Carmichael Oh.

Billie (*to Reg and Geraldine*) Do you remember what my mother and father were like in those days?

Reg (*looking at Geraldine*) Yes I do.

Geraldine (*looking at him*) So do I.

Billie Well it was very lucky for them I wasn't taken into care! My parents were hippies, Mr Beamish.

Mr Beamish (*shocked*) Good God!

Billie Yes and so were all their friends. Our house was always full of loud music and peculiar people and we never had regular meals and my PE kit was always getting lost. And they took me to political rallies and they shouted horrible, rude things to policemen and once they made me go to a rock concert with them and it rained and our tent leaked. And they were always having rows and throwing things and they wouldn't let me join the Brownies and the electricity was always getting cut off because they forgot to pay the bill not to speak of my pocket money which I hardly ever got. And our house was always a terrible mess because the charlady was a recovered mental patient only she wasn't. And the only normal person in my life was my grandmother because she always did what she said she was going to do and she never forgot things and you knew what the rules were. And furthermore (*with sudden passionate rage*) she knits! Which my mother would never even try to learn!

Mr Beamish I'm very sorry to hear all this. A sad and terrible story. A deplorable upbringing.

Bunny Oh I don't know . . .

Mrs Carmichael (*springing forward*) Now Billie, we don't want to give Mr Beamish a wrong impression. After all, your parents were victims of the Permissive Society. What could they do against Flower Power and militant art colleges and that Jagger person? They were helpless.

Billie Granny!

Mrs Carmichael (*ignoring her; to Mr Beamish*) And, of course, Reginald and Geraldine have changed out of all recognition since those ... (*She falters*)

Reg (*helpfully*) Changed?

Geraldine In what way, Mrs C?

Mrs Carmichael (*fixing her eyes on Mr Beamish, her voice getting louder*) They've made a new life for themselves out here in the Green Belt, a happy, harmonious home. Settled down. Active in the community. In short, Mr Beamish, in spite of their somewhat carefree past they have become sensible, law-abiding citizens who, although they may not actually vote Tory, are basically and at heart and at the end of the day, a good solid conservative couple of whom our Prime Minister would be proud!

Reg Hoorah!

Geraldine Absolutely bang on, Mrs C!

Mrs Carmichael (*turning on them*) I was not talking about you!

Billie You weren't talking about anybody. I'm amazed at you, Granny.

Mrs Carmichael (*fighting for calm*) Billie, I am simply trying to ... (*She sags and turns away. She goes and gets herself a glass of brandy*)

Bunny I thought Islington sounded terrific, Billie.

Billie (*coldly*) Oh did you? (*She marches over to where she put his spectacles and gets them*)

Mr Beamish (*to Bunny*) I trust you're not saying that you admire that kind of lifestyle.

Bunny But we both do, Dad. Now. Forgetting about convention. Breaking the rules ... that's what you and I——

Billie hands him his spectacles

Oh, you found them.

Reg Billie!

Geraldine What are you doing?

Billie I think Bunny's gone without his glasses long enough tonight.

Bunny Maybe you're right. (*He starts to put them on*)

Reg breaks into sudden loud sobs

Aunt Lillian, what's wrong? (*He puts his spectacles down*)

Mr Beamish What is it?

Reg Oh I know it's silly of me but it was Aggie talking about what a wonderful couple Reg and Gerry are. And look at Rollo and me!

Billie (*to Bunny*) Yes do. (*She tries to hand him his spectacles again*)

Geraldine (*a menacing lunge at Reg*) Still hankering to be a battered wife, eh Lillian?

Bunny Wait a minute! (*He gets between them*)

Geraldine I suppose she's been telling you I'm an unspeakable bounder.

Reg (*hiding behind Mr Beamish*) I haven't said one single word against you, have I, Mr Beamish?

Mr Beamish (*sternly*) Not a word. Though God knows she has cause.

Bunny Cause? Why? What has he done to her? (*To Geraldine*) Listen
    you——

Geraldine Oh I see. She's got everybody on her side again. Little Miss
    Victim. God, if only Gerry was here! She'd understand. (*To Mrs
    Carmichael*) Where's she got to?

Mrs Carmichael (*backing away*) What?

Geraldine Gerry. She should have been down by now. Where is she?

Mrs Carmichael Down? What? Who?

Geraldine What's the matter, wax in your ears? (*Shouting*) Where's Geral-
    dine?

Mrs Carmichael I don't know, I don't know! Get away from me!

Mr Beamish Leave her alone. A poor defenceless old woman.

Mrs Carmichael (*furiously*) Old!

Reg You see? I told you. Gerry is the only one he wants.

Geraldine Much good it does me. She's crazy about Reg.

Reg (*after a brief pause*) She is?

Geraldine Mad about him . . . God knows why.

Billie Bunny, this is the last thing I'll ever ask you to do for me. (*She gives
    him the spectacles*)

Bunny All right, Billie . . . what do you mean, the last?

Geraldine (*putting the spectacles into his pocket*) It's all very well for you,
    Boyo. You're young. I've had twenty years with Lillian . . . millstone
    round my neck.

Mr Beamish Millstone? She's a very unhappy woman.

Geraldine Unhappy, Stanley? She's round the bend. What? Roller skating
    through Fortnum and Masons, kissograms to the Pope, graffiti at
    Number Ten——

Billie Bunny, will you please put these on!

*She gets the spectacles out and gives them to him. He puts them on. She points
at Reg and Geraldine*

There!

He stares. His mouth drops open. They stare silently back

And I never want to see you again!

Billie runs out of the room

Bunny (*still staring*) Don't go, Billie.

Mr Beamish What is the matter with you, Bun?

Bunny (*slowly*) Am I out of my mind?

Reg (*with sudden melodrama*) No! I am! That's why Rollo hates me! I'm just
    a burden to him and a burden to the world. I can't bear it any longer, I
    can't I can't I can't! I'm going to kill myself! Goodbye, Rollo. No! Don't
    try and stop me! I'm going to the station and throw myself under a train!

Reg rushes sobbing out and we hear the front door slam

Mr Beamish After her, Bun! Stop her!

Bunny I have to see Billie.

Mr Beamish (*rushing him out*) Hurry!
Bunny I've got to talk to Billie!
Mr Beamish This is an emergency. Go! Go! (*He turns to Geraldine*) Where is the station?

Bunny goes

Geraldine Just down at the bottom of the road.
Mr Beamish Oh my God! (*He starts out, then stops*) Aren't you coming?
Geraldine No thanks. I think I'll sit this one out. Better make it snappy, Stanley. There's an express in four minutes.
Mr Beamish You swine! (*To Mrs Carmichael*) Come on.
Mrs Carmichael No!
Mr Beamish Yes!
Mrs Carmichael I won't!
Mr Beamish You'll do as I say!
Mrs Carmichael (*rather pleased*) Oh.

Mr Beamish rushes Mrs Carmichael out

There is the sound of the front door opening and closing behind them

Reg comes trotting in from the kitchen

He stops. He and Geraldine look at each other

Geraldine (*folding her arms*) Well, I hope you're enjoying yourself.
Reg You bet. Aren't you?
Geraldine (*loftily*) Certainly not. I am simply trying to straighten things out.
Reg (*walking towards her*) Is that so?
Geraldine You were making such a mess of it all I had to do something.
Reg (*still advancing*) Rollo to the rescue, eh?
Geraldine Throw yourself under a train! That station's been closed for years.

By now they are standing very close and looking at each other

Reg I wanted to talk to you.
Geraldine My mother says I should divorce you.
Reg She says Lillian should be certified.
Geraldine Quite right. Lillian's a raving nutcase.
Reg Only because Rollo's an unspeakable bounder.
Geraldine No he isn't. He's just lonely.
Reg Lillian's been lonely for years.
Geraldine Poor Lillian.
Reg Poor Rollo.

They look at each other in silence for a moment

Billie comes in from the front hall unseen by either of them. She's carrying a suitcase and she stands watching them

You said Gerry was crazy about Reg. Is that true?
Geraldine I don't know. It was just something to say.

Reg Take off that moustache.
Geraldine Why should I?
Reg Because I say so. Take it off.
Geraldine No. (*She pauses*) Oh all right.

She takes it off and Reg, very gently, kisses her on the lips

(*After the kiss*) Gerry's crazy about Reg.

They put their arms around each other and kiss again. Billie, watches, smiling

Reg Oh Gerry, you're the most marvellous woman in the world.
Geraldine (*laughing*) Not as marvellous as you. Mrs Blick!
Reg (*laughing too*) Your mother's face!

Bunny comes in quietly from the kitchen

He doesn't see Billie but she sees him and ducks out of sight. Bunny clears his throat. Reg and Geraldine turn and see him

Bunny I saw you running back to the house, Aunt Lillian ... I mean——
Reg Reg.
Bunny (*shaking his hand*) How do you do. I feel like a total fool.
Geraldine Oh Bunny, no.

Billie appears again behind them but none of them see her

Bunny I don't know where Billie got the idea you were bored with each other. (*Miserably*) And I don't know why she's so angry with me.
Reg It's us she's angry with.
Bunny No. She said she hated me. I don't know what I'll do if I lose Billie. I can't live without her.

In the background Billie beams

I'd marry her in twenty churches if only she wouldn't leave me.

The doorbell rings

Billie (*coolly*) I'll get it.

They all stare at her

Bunny Billie!

She goes out to the door. Mr Beamish enters in a rage followed by a breathless Mrs Carmichael, and then Billie

Mr Beamish I've been made a fool of! I have run shouting through the streets ... (*To Reg*) You're here! (*Then even angrier*) I have been to a derelict railway station ... (*He stares at Geraldine*) Mr Stringer! What has happened to your moustache?

There is a catastrophic pause

(*With ill-controlled fury*) I would like an explanation!
Billie (*calmly*) Mr Beamish.

He looks at her

Uncle Rollo has just shaved it off.

Mr Beamish (*sharply*) What?

Billie (*smiling*) For Aunt Lillian. She always hated that moustache. You've brought them back together, Mr Beamish.

Reg and Geraldine look at Billie with pleasure and surprise. Mr Beamish looks at them without any expression. Then, slowly, he breaks into a smile

Mr Beamish Is this true?

Reg (*in Lillian's voice*) It is it is it is, Mr Beamish! And all due to you. You've simply transformed us! Rollo says he sees me in a new light and he's sorry for everything.

Geraldine (*in Rollo's voice; sincere*) And I must apologize to you too, Stanley . . . forgive me—Mr Beamish. I've been unmannerly and boorish and I ask your pardon. Quite frankly, I was mad with jealousy. But when I realized that what you felt for my Lillian was compassion and respect. (*She hangs her head*) I was ashamed.

Bunny is suddenly overcome with laughter

Mr Beamish (*very displeased*) Bun. This is a solemn moment. (*He turns back to Geraldine and Reg*) Mr Stringer, your apology is generous and manly. I accept it. (*He pauses*) Do you love your wife?

Geraldine (*just succeeding in not laughing*) I do.

Mr Beamish (*gently to Reg*) And you, Aunt Lillian, can you love this man?

Reg (*with an effortful straight face*) Yes I can, Mr Beamish. I do.

Mr Beamish takes their hands and joins them

Mr Beamish My blessings on you both.

They kiss chastely

Geraldine Come, Lillian, we must get our things and go back to our own little home.

Reg Yes, Rollo.

Hand in hand they go out together

After they're gone Mr Beamish takes out his handkerchief and blows his nose. Mrs Carmichael gets up and strides purposefully to the hall

Mr Beamish Where are you going?

Mrs Carmichael (*in cold fury*) I am going to speak to them.

Mr Beamish You are not. I forbid it!

Mrs Carmichael I am. You can't stop me.

Mr Beamish Mrs Carmichael, this is not the moment.

Mrs Carmichael Oh yes it is!

Mrs Carmichael goes

Mr Beamish starts after her. Then he stops and shakes his head, indulgently

Mr Beamish A real bucking bronco of a woman. Needs taming of course. Now Bun, have you had your little talk with Miss Stringer?

Bunny No, Dad.

Mr Beamish Then I will leave you in private.

Billie Don't go, Mr Beamish. Bunny and I can say all we have to say in front of you. It won't take long.

Bunny Listen to me, Bllie.

Billie No Bunny, you listen to me. I'm not going to marry you.

Mr Beamish (*nodding*) Correct.

Bunny (*in despair*) Don't say that, Billie, please! Don't say it!

Mr Beamish What's this? What's this?

Mrs Carmichael reappears looking disconcerted

Mrs Carmichael They've locked the bedroom door.

Billie smiles delightedly but as Bunny looks at her, she converts it into a frown

Mr Beamish Not surprising. They have much to talk about. Now Bun, pull yourself together please. You seem confused.

Bunny I am. Billie, if it's bridesmaids and page boys and——

Billie It's too late for all that now, Bunny. I'm sorry but I'm not going to marry you.

Mrs Carmichael What! What are you talking about? Have you gone mad?

Mr Beamish Mrs Carmichael, be silent!

Mrs Carmichael (*frenzied*) I won't. Why should I? Have I gone through all this for nothing? This has been the most terrible night of my life.

Mr Beamish It's been a difficult evening for us all. Now kindly let us get these matters straight. Bun, did you or did you not say to me this evening in this very room that you did not wish to marry Miss Stringer.

Bunny Yes I did, but——

Mrs Carmichael (*savagely*) We'll sue you for breach of promise!

Mr Beamish Madam!

Mrs Carmichael Don't "madam" me, Mr Beamish. I want to know what's——

Mr Beamish Sit down.

She does

Leave this to me. (*He turns to Billie*) Miss Stringer, do you mean what you said?

Billie I do!

Mr Beamish You do not wish to marry my son?

Billie I don't.

Mrs Carmichael moans. Bunny starts to leave the room

Bunny I can't stand this. I'm leaving.

Billie Wait, Bunny.

Mr Beamish Yes, calm down, lad. Be thankful that all this has been settled so amicably. Miss Stringer, you are a brave soldier. When I told you that Bun had confided in me about wanting to break off the relationship——

Bunny Wanting to what? I never said that!

Mr Beamish You did! No engagement, you said, and no marriage. In this room. To me.

Billie And now I'm saying it too. (*She pauses. She beams at Bunny*) But I will live with you, Bunny.

Mrs Carmichael (*a scream*) Billie!

Mr Beamish Miss Stringer! Consider your modesty!

Bunny Billie, you will?

She nods, smiling

Oh my God, it's too good to be true.

Billie I love you, Bunny. I think you're the most marvellous man in the world.

Bunny I'm not, I'm not. But I love you, Billie.

They kiss each other

Mrs Carmichael Stop that this instant! I forbid it!

Mr Beamish You forbid it! Society forbids it!

Reg comes in dressed as himself

Reg What ho, everybody! Sorry to have missed so much of the party. Touch of migraine. But I've had a little nap and I feel like a new man.

Mr Beamish Stringer! Speak to your daughter!

Reg Hello, Billie.

Billie (*very affectionately*) Hello, Daddy.

Reg You must be Bun.

Bunny (*laughing*) And you must be Reg.

Reg I think I must.

Mr Beamish Stringer, please! We have a crisis here.

Mrs Carmichael Where is Geraldine?

Geraldine comes in dressed in the sequin sleeveless, looking wonderful

Geraldine Here I am.

Billie Mother, Bunny and I are going to live together.

Geraldine Oh darling, how wonderful. (*She hugs her*) But wouldn't you rather get married?

Reg Well? Wouldn't you, Billie?

Billie Well . . . (*She goes over to Bunny*) Will you marry me, Bunny?

Bunny Will I!

Reg (*going out*) I'll get the champagne.

Reg goes to the kitchen

Mr Beamish Thank God!

Mrs Carmichael Billie, dear! Good girl.

Reg returns and pours out the champagne during the following

Mr Beamish Mrs Stringer, you saved these children from a fate worse than death. Isn't that so, Mrs Carmichael?

Mrs Carmichael (*grudgingly*) Yes. (*She pauses*) Well done, Geraldine.
Geraldine (*demurely*) Thank you, Mother.

Reg hands round the champagne

Mr Beamish A happy ending, eh Mrs Carmichael? Or may I call you
    Agatha?
Mrs Carmichael Of course ... Stanley.
Mr Beamish But Aunt Lillian and Uncle Rollo must join us for the toast.

A pause. Everyone looks at everyone else and then looks away

Geraldine Gone home, Mr Beamish! Just slipped quietly away. So happy
    and peaceful. A miracle. I don't know how you did it.
Mr Beamish (*complacently*) Well well ... just two lost children waiting to be
    shown the path. May I say you look quite lovely in that dress, Mrs
    Stringer? A vision of delight!
Geraldine Thank you, Mr Beamish. (*She looks round him to smile trium-*
    phantly at her mother)
Mrs Carmichael (*raising her glass*) To Billie and Bunny!
Billie No Granny, first we should drink to Rollo and Lillian.
Bunny
Billie
Mr Beamish   } (*together*) To Rollo and Lillian!
Mrs Carmichael
Reg (*to Geraldine*) To Rollo.
Geraldine (*to him*) To Lillian.

Music

CURTAIN

FURNITURE AND PROPERTY LIST

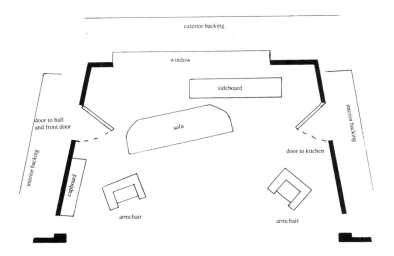

ACT I

On stage: Sofa. *Behind it:* black plastic bag containing sports jacket and skirt
Two armchairs
Cupboard
Sideboard. *On it:* decanters, bottles of spirits, liqueurs, etc., glasses, bowl of nuts, telephone, clock
Mirror and pictures on walls
Carpet
Practical vacuum cleaner
Curtains at window open

Off stage: Glass of water **(Geraldine)**
Frozen turkey in pan **(Mrs Carmichael)**
Pot plants **(Billie)**
Papers, tea cosy **(Reg)**
Briefcase **(Geraldine)**
Briefcase **(Mr Beamish)**
Bottle of marsala **(Reg)**
Bag of golf clubs **(Reg)**
Plate of canapés **(Geraldine)**

Personal: **Mrs Carmichael:** wrist-watch (required throughout), handbag containing
              pills, notebook, pen, brown wig, blue-rinse wig, scarf
              Mr Beamish: paper and pen in pocket, key

ACT II

On stage: As before

Off stage: Coffee tray **(Geraldine)**
              Spectacles **(Billie)**
              Cardigan **(Geraldine)**
              White cardigan **(Geraldine)**
              Cup of sugar **(Reg)**
              Bottle of champagne **(Reg)**

Personal: **Mr Beamish:** handkerchief

LIGHTING PLOT

Practical fittings required: pendant light

Interior: a living-room. The same scene throughout

ACT I

To open: Black-out

ACT II

To open: General interior lighting with practical on

No cues

EFFECTS PLOT

ACT I

Cue 1   To open   (Page 1)
Music: "Strike Up the Band"

Cue 2   The Lights come up   (Page 1)
Fade music

Cue 3   **Mrs Carmichael:** "It's the least I can do, child."   (Page 6)
Taxi honks

Cue 4   The Lights fade to Black-out   (Page 8)
Music; fade when ready

Cue 5   **Geraldine:** "Reg——"   (Page 11)
Front door slams

Cue 6   The Lights fade to Black-out   (Page 11)
Music; fade when ready

Cue 7   **Billie** goes out through the kitchen   (Page 12)
Back door opens and closes

Cue 8   **Geraldine** sings   (Page 12)
Front door opens

Cue 9   **Reg:** "Oh absolutely positive."   (Page 12)
Front door closes

Cue 10   **Geraldine:** "She may be back."   (Page 13)
Telephone

Cue 11   **Reg:** "Archaic!"   (Page 13)
Telephone

Cue 12   **Reg:** "Yes of course. Certainly."   (Page 14)
Back door opens and closes

Cue 13   **Reg:** ". . . they ought to be ashamed of themselves."   (Page 22)
Telephone

Cue 14   **Geraldine:** ". . . straight home to bed and——"   (Page 23)
Front door opens and closes

Cue 15   **Mr Beamish:** "These are reading glasses."   (Page 24)
Sound from the kitchen

ACT II

Cue 16   To open Act II   (Page 27)
Music; fade when ready

MADE AND PRINTED IN GREAT BRITAIN BY
LATIMER TREND & COMPANY LTD PLYMOUTH

MADE IN ENGLAND